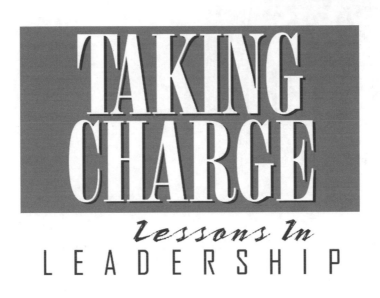

TAKING CHARGE

Lessons In

LEADERSHIP

Insight Publishing Company
Sevierville, Tennessee

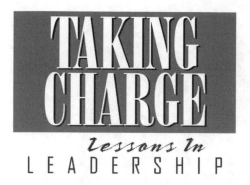

© 2003 by Insight Publishing Company.

Published by Insight Publishing Company
P.O. Box 4189
Sevierville, Tennessee 37864

Cover design and book layout by Russ Hollingsworth.
Edited by Amanda Maples.

Printed in the United States of America

ISBN: 1-885640-13-7

Contents

A Message From The Publisher

"Before you can inspire with emotion, you must be swamped with it yourself. Before you can move their tears, your own must flow. To convince them, you must yourself believe."

Winston Churchill

The mere fact that you are holding this book and reading this page says something about you. You must be a leader, aspire to become a leader or, at the very least, are curious about what makes a leader tick. You are, in fact, a rarity in this world, because real, honest-to-goodness leaders are not found on every street corner or behind every desk.

Real leaders are unique. They think differently. They see their world and their role in it differently. Most people see a problem and form an opinion. A leader sees a problem and begins formulating a plan. Most people wonder what their purpose is in life. A leader already knows.

I'm not saying that leadership is easy. In fact, it is not only difficult, it is often lonely and frustrating. Leaders are not perfect. Their flaws gnaw at them and at times bring them to ruin. But leaders never quit leading, and they should never quit learning about themselves and about leadership in an ever-changing world.

Taking Charge: Lessons In Leadership is a collection of conversations from some of America's most dynamic leaders. Their insights, perspectives, and strategies are having a dramatic impact on people, organizations, and even countries, across America and around the world. You will learn from these leaders and find encouragement and inspiration to continue your own leadership journey. It is a journey well worth taking.

Russ Hollingsworth

Chapter 1

WARREN BENNIS

Warren Bennis has written or edited twenty-seven books, including the best-selling Leaders *and* On Becoming A Leader, *both of which have been trans-lated into twenty-one languages. He has served on four U.S. presidential advisory boards and has consulted for many Fortune 500 companies, including General Electric, Ford and Starbucks.* The Wall Street Journal *named him one of the top ten speakers on management in 1993 and 1996, and* Forbes *magazine referred to him as "the dean of leadership gurus."*

David E. Wright (Wright)

It is my sincere pleasure to be speaking with Dr. Warren G. Bennis. Dr. Bennis is a Distinguished Professor of Business Administration and founding chairman of the Leadership Institute at the University of Southern California. He also serves as chairman of the advisory board for the Center for Public Leadership at Harvard University's John F. Kennedy School of Government, and he is the Thomas S. Murphy Distinguished Research Fellow at the Harvard Business School. In addition to his books, Dr. Bennis has written more than 2,000 articles, which have appeared in the *Harvard Business Review, Fast Company* magazine, *The New York Times, Atlantic Monthly, The Wall Street Journal, Psychology Today* and numerous management-related publications. Dr. Bennis, it's an honor to talk with you.

Dr. Warren Bennis (Bennis)

Thank you, David.

Wright

I don't know how comfortable you are with labels like genius, guru and legend, but it is a fact that many of our readers consider you such. However, in the rare event that one of them is meeting you for the first time, would you offer us a brief overview of the high points of your life and career? In other words, how did your life's path bring you to this place?

Bennis

It's always difficult to answer those questions, because as you look back, you try to look for a pattern. I think, in my case, there were many eccentric precursors that led to where I am today. Being in the army in World War II was certainly a significant experience as was leading a platoon of infantry-men in Germany when I was nineteen. One of the men in my platoon used to talk about a college that he wanted to go to—Antioch College in Yellow Springs, Ohio. I had never heard of the college or the town, but I wound up going there because they had a co-op program in which you worked part of the year and went to school part of the year. That was my introduction to the idea of how you can bridge and yoke together theory and practice. You were in a classroom for twelve weeks, then working for twelve weeks, and then you returned to campus. You were always on a tightrope between the world of practice and the world of theory, research and intellectual inquiry. That was one of the reasons college was such a profound experience; I learned that there was nothing as practical as a good theory. The other reason was that the college's president, Dr. Douglas McGregor, was the founder of the field of organizational behavior and leadership back in the '40s. He was my role model.

After college, I went to MIT, where I founded a group that was very serious about the field of leadership and organization. We started a department there, which was probably one of the first of its kind in the country, if not the world. I took my work/study idea seriously, and after being an academic for about twenty years, I decided to become a university president, which I did for about seven years. I ended up teaching, writing and consulting at the University of Southern California. That's roughly how I got from there to here.

Wright

Dr. Bennis, I spent some time this week on Amazon.com just scrolling through all the titles you've authored, co-authored or edited. It's a stagger-ing collection. Of all the books that you've written, are there any that stand out in your mind as life markers for you or books that changed your life in significant ways?

Bennis

I don't know if they changed my life, but if I could be bold and audacious, I hope they've been able to change other people's lives somewhat. I think there are two or three books that I would like to underscore. My first book, *The Planning of Change*, was co-edited and co-authored with two of my mentors, Ken Benne and Bob Chin. It was a book of readings we compiled and long essays that we wrote, and I'm very proud of it, because it laid some of the groundwork for organizational and institutional change. It was published in 1961, at a time when there was not much literature on the subject, so I'm proud of that book. Another title I would mention, *On Becoming A Leader*, is the one that I enjoyed writing most, and it's the one that I assign to my students, whether they're executives, high school students or undergraduates. It has been recently revised and is my personal statement about leadership. Finally, the book that I co-authored with Bob Thomas, *Geeks and Geezers*, has been recently published. It is about leaders age thirty-two and younger and leaders age seventy and older, and it compares the effects that two different eras have had on leadership. In my case, I'm a "geezer," and the most influential events in my experience were the Depression and World War II. We compared a group with that background to the "geeks" group, who were born in the late '60s and '70s, and studied how those two groups differed. In the course of writing that book, we learned a great deal about how leaders develop, how people extract wisdom from experience and how people continue to grow despite their age.

Wright

Geeks and Geezers is one of the most unique titles I've ever read. At first glance, I thought, "Boy, this is not worthy of Bennis!" Then I read the subtitle, which adds significant context to the title: *How Era, Values and Defining Moments Shape Leaders*. It's a fascinating book. What led you to write it, and where did the idea come from?

Bennis

Two factors triggered the idea. First, I was interested in the generation that's grown up in the last twenty years or so. Right now, they're between the ages of twenty-two and thirty-two. In this country, there are more than eighty million people in that particular group. That's a bigger spike in population than we saw with the Baby Boomer generation. This is a group that's grown up "virtual, digital and visual." Many of these people had computers when they were in the first grade or kindergarten. That has to have affected the way they look at the world. They've grown up during a period of uninterrupted prosperity and in a time of options. They've also grown up in a time of U.S. hegemony. There's no question that we are now the single power in the world, far beyond what England was in the nineteenth century, when it ruled the waves. So I was interested in trying to understand this generation—their minds, their thoughts, their philosophies.

I was also interested in geezers, people like me, seventy years and older, who keep reinventing themselves, who keep their eyebrows raised in curiosity, who keep doing things that are exciting and interesting. Why do they do that, and what can we learn about these elders who seem to retain youthful characteristics way into old age? Those were the reasons I became interested in doing the book.

Wright

You discuss how great leaders in these two generations are often transformed in their very personal crucibles.

Bennis

What we really got out of this work was hearing people talk about those events in their lives that transformed them—their crucible experiences. In fact, I sometimes wish we had called the book *Leadership Crucibles*.

Wright

Can you give us an example that might help our readers understand what a crucible experience is?

Bennis

Being in a crucible is like when you're in a vortex of adversity, of challenge—often a loss of some kind. I'll give you several examples. Mike Wallace, founder of the television show *60 Minutes*, said that the crucible experience in his life was when his nineteen-year-old son, Peter, fell off a mountaintop in Greece and died. Wallace said at the time that it changed his life. He said, "Now I'm going to do what I really want to do," so he started *60 Minutes*.

Another example would be eighty-five-year-old Sidney Rittenberg, who is now running a consulting business in Seattle and helping U.S. companies develop businesses in China. Sidney, who ended up in China during World

War II, became an advisor to Mao Tse Tung, Chou En-Lai and other Chinese leaders. Following the Cultural Revolution, these same leaders imprisoned him for thirteen or fourteen years. When he finally returned to the states in 1981, he became an entrepreneur. That experience of being in prison for all those years during the Cultural Revolution was what shaped him.

There's the case of Jeff Wilke, who's now a senior executive at Amazon.com. When he was working for AlliedSignal, a factory under his supervision burned down, and several people were killed. Wilke had to spend the better part of a week talking to their surviving family members. He realized as a result of that experience how important human life was, how business wasn't just about meeting the quarterly earnings report, that running a corporation was very much like being part of a community. It changed his whole outlook on leadership and management.

Then there's the story of Tara Church, who is now in her third year at Harvard Law School. When she was eight years old, Tara and her Brownie troop were on a weekend hiking trip in the Los Angeles area. There was a drought in Los Angeles at the time, so the girls decided to take paper plates along, because they didn't want to use water to wash the plates and the other equipment they had. Then they realized that paper plates were made from wood, and they became worried about the deforestation going on throughout the world. Tara Church and about six or seven of her fellow Brownies started an organization in which groups of Brownies all over the country would start planting trees to make up for the trees lost to deforestation. They called themselves the Tree Musketeers, and it's now a national organization. Tara's mother is chairman of the board. They have an executive running it and plant about a million trees a year.

Wright

Dr. Bennis, many of our listeners work for companies that are struggling to cope with change. Individually, of course, it's a daunting task for professionals to change with the times, to adopt new ways of thinking or working. In my experience, it seems that it's almost unnatural for human beings to change significantly. What are your recommendations for helping people to move out of their comfort zones and to embrace change?

Bennis

That's a big and important question. I don't think change is necessarily something that's resisted at all times by all people. I think, in some cases, there are people who really anticipate, look forward to and thrive on change. And in this world, if they don't, they're going to miss the train. There's not an institution that I know, not a profession that I'm aware of, that isn't undergoing constant and spastic change. Change is now the constant. Even though it may not be a natural act for certain people, I think it's something that everyone has got to understand. Take education, for example. It's no longer just four years of college. Education is really turning into a process of lifelong learning. Universities are going to have to take responsibility not just for their alumni but for people in much older age groups, who have to keep learning because the half-life of professions is shrinking every day.

The way organizations must deal with change is by helping people realize that in the process of changing they're going to benefit from all sorts of educational programs and opportunities. The people have to be *involved* in the change, because if they are a part of the process, they're much less threatened by change. There are a lot of reasons why most people resist change, but among the most important is their reliance on old habits, especially the ones that have been successful. Related to that is self-esteem. If you're doing something extremely well, are pretty successful at it, getting a lot of rewards for it and your sense of self-esteem is based on your competence, it's got to be difficult if you're put into a totally different and new situation. Organizations have to help people get into a safe "holding pattern" where they can learn new skills without it being a threat to their self-esteem. So to summarize, people have got to be *involved* in the change, they have got to be *informed* of the change, and they have got to be *educated* and put into a *safe holding area* where they're not going to be overly threatened by change.

Wright

I've noted that some leaders want to grow and improve. They've read about philosophies and strategies, but they strike out with ideas that are untested. How do you think an organization can ensure that it's getting the right kind of help before implementing new strategic initiatives?

Bennis

There are some vaunted organizations with good track records that can help out—the Conference Board, the American Management Association and a number of business schools and consulting firms, for example. They've already been "vetted," so to speak. If you were interested in finance, you would probably want help from places like Carnegie Mellon or the Wharton School or Stanford. If you're interested in overall management, you might want to bring in somebody from the Harvard Business School. There are also journals like the *Harvard Business Review*, the *MIT Sloan Management Review* and *Organization Dynamics* that people can read.

However, as a consultant, I have found that the problems presented to me are often too vague or not very clear. So the first thing a company should do, even before thinking about looking for a consultant, is identify which issues it needs help with. But I would like to add one more thing: There's usually enough wisdom and enough people in an organization who have the knowledge and the understanding to help solve a particular problem before seeking a consultant. One of the most important attributes of leadership is understanding and developing that talent. I really think that most people and most organizations have the inherent competence to solve their own problems without going outside.

Wright

In the late '70s and early '80s, I was writing a training course for a national franchise, and it was based on objectives. In almost everything that I read while preparing the course material, the author was either commenting on something that you had written or just outright saying it himself. Did you have anything to do with management by objectives?

Bennis

The idea of management by objectives belongs to Peter Drucker. My own mentor, Doug McGregor, is another person who was very keen on the idea of not just management by objectives but the whole issue of "personnel evaluation." To work with the person you're trying to supervise, help, develop or coach was to work out the objectives together. Even today, if you were to say to Peter Drucker, "Leadership is important," he would ask, "Leadership for what?" There's always an objective for everything we should be doing.

Wright

With the complexity of today's business culture, how important is it for a leader to know how to measure the effectiveness of his strategies for growth and change?

Bennis

It's always useful to have metrics that really make a difference and to measure those as much as possible. The problem with metrics is that they are often too narrow, as with exclusively financial metrics. Often those things that are easier to measure mislead us because of the "fallacy of concreteness." For example, a company's earnings might seem concrete, but these days, even earnings are being questioned. The number of companies restating their earnings is extraordinarily high right now. So it depends on what metrics you're talking about, because some things are best understood through anecdotal or qualitative methods.

The important question to ask is, "What are the metrics that really make a difference?" For example, if we're going to look at organizations, we have to realize that they are also communities. So we wouldn't want to just measure financial results. In the long run, we might want to measure such things as the general climate of the organization or how much stress is present or how many opportunities for growth and development there are or how innovative the company is. We must also develop metrics for understanding how transparent an organization is. How much candor is there among employees? These are hard things to measure, but they can be more critical than short-term financial results. In fact, I believe that metrics like those have to augment quarterly reports on earnings. I'm not saying or advocating that earnings or financial data are not important; in the long run, of course, they have to be important.

Wright

A lot has been written about the rise and fall of technology companies in recent years. There are other glaring examples of poor leadership at the corporate level that have resulted in the bankruptcies of some of the nation's largest companies. It's as if many of these highly successful organizations never really understood what made them successful and, therefore, they couldn't replicate their success when the economy or the culture changed.

Bennis

I think that's absolutely true.

Wright

From your experience, what is the single most important consideration for companies seeking successful organizational change and improving results from their efforts?

Bennis

There are two major indicators by which organizations can be measured. They are my two big "A's." The first big "A" is alignment. How aligned is an organization? That is, at every level of the hierarchy, how are people aligned behind the mission and the vision and the strategy of the organization? Are the main driving mission and strategy understood at every single level? Are they acted on, and are they rewarded? The second "A" is adaptability, the extent to which an organization has the capacity to be agile, to be quick to take advantage of opportunities. The real trick of leadership, then, is getting an organization aligned behind changing strategies and missions. You see, if you just have alignment without adaptability, you've got an old-fashioned command-and-control, almost militaristic, organization. If you just have adaptability without alignment, you have a sort of anarchy in which no one knows what's going on. Both have to be yoked together, and leadership has to somehow create alignment with adaptability.

Wright

What a great half-hour this has been. Dr. Bennis, I really appreciate the time that you spent with me today.

Bennis

It was my pleasure, David. Thank you very much.

Wright

Today we've been talking with Dr. Warren G. Bennis, who is a distinguished professor of business administration at the Marshall School of Business and founding chairman of the Leadership Institute, both at the University of Southern California. He served for many years on the faculties of the Sloan School of Management at MIT, Harvard Business School and Boston University.

Warren Bennis
m.christian@marshall.usc.edu

Chapter 2

GARY A. GARNER

Gary Garner is a speaker and consultant on leadership, customer service, creativity and management. He is also a successful speaking coach. For more than twenty years, Gary has perfected the skills and techniques that he now shares with others, researching and applying techniques that anyone can use to develop and enhance personal creativity. Gary draws on his experiences to teach, motivate and inspire others to develop their leadership skills.

David E. Wright (Wright)

Today we're talking to Gary Garner, who is a professional speaker and consultant. He has spent more than thirty years working in the public and private sectors. As an administrator, Gary worked to develop leadership skills in others. He has mentored and taught leadership classes to hundreds of people over that time, sharing lessons that he's learned from history, research and hands-on experience. Gary has developed, implemented and managed successful billion-dollar projects affecting millions of people. Gary takes great pride in the fact that many of these supervisors and managers have gone on to become effective leaders themselves. Gary, welcome to *Taking Charge.*

Gary Garner (Garner)

Thank you, David.

Wright

After all these years of research on leadership, where do you think someone should begin if he or she wants to get started on the road to taking charge as a leader?

Garner

There are two key points at which to start. First, you have to start with yourself. Second, you have to develop an action plan and commit to it. Let me discuss each of these. We'll begin with the first point. Before you decide to take charge of someone else, you have to take charge of yourself. Thousands of years ago, the Oracle at Delphi gave management advice that is valid today: "Know thyself." Look at the task you want to undertake and ask yourself if you have the discipline it will take to accomplish that task. What are the risks, and are you physically, mentally and financially willing to take them? Are you committed enough to overcome the inertia that fights change, to overcome the doubts that will arise within yourself and to overcome the negative reinforcement you may get from others? In other words, make sure you fully understand the task and the challenges, and then determine if you believe in this cause enough to finish the task. Do you believe in yourself and your abilities? When some people hear the phrase, "Do you believe?" they may think it is only a religious question, but I'm talking about whether or not you have enough faith in yourself to undertake what you're contemplating. Some people refer to this idea as the Pygmalion Effect, named after a Greek sculptor who created a beautiful marble sculpture of a woman, fell in love with her and then believed in her so strongly that she became real. You may not be trying to turn stone into the perfect woman, but the point of this Greek myth was to reinforce to the Greek populace that they could accomplish impossible things if they truly believe in them. Modern psychologists also refer to the concept of believing as a "self-fulfilling prophecy." If you have truly internalized the belief in yourself that you can do something, you are more likely to succeed. If you believe you can't, you won't succeed. As Henry Ford put it, "Whether you think you can or think you can't—you're right." This strong sense of belief and confidence is one of the characteristics that contribute to successful leaders. People will not follow someone who does not believe in himself and doesn't believe he can accomplish the goal. Can you imagine the reaction of soldiers to an officer who said, "Sorry, guys. I don't think we can take that hill, but I'd like you to go anyway; I'll wait here for you"? Needless to say, a coach would be fired if he told his team, "I believe we're going to have a losing season this year. I'm not a very good coach, and none of you have much skill." In fact, we want coaches who not only believe they can win but who reinforce that belief with everything they do.

Please note that I said that you have to analyze and understand the physical, mental and emotional aspects required for the task. I am also suggesting that success will be based on analysis and understanding, not just "believing." To put it mildly, it would indicate a serious lack of analysis and preparation for the task if someone simply said, "I believe I can fly" and jumped off a building. But if the person took hang gliding lessons and had a hang glider strapped to his back, then he has a good chance of achieving that long-sought dream of soaring like a bird.

There are many critical issues in our world that need taking charge of, but there is a symptom that afflicts many people in our society, and that is the opposite of believing in yourself. That affliction is what I call the "victim mentality." It shows up in all kinds of groups and individuals and seems to freeze them like a deer in headlights on a dark country road. And just like the deer, they stand there afraid to do anything and get run over. If they survive, they and their fellow "victim mentality" cohorts will say being run over only reinforces that they were right in believing they could not cross the road.

Let's examine some of the psychological issues related to taking charge. Our basic psychological make-up seems to be to resist change and then to immediately start rationalizing why it is better not to change. You cannot convince others to support and follow you if you are not totally convinced yourself. Although some people may not believe mechanical lie detectors work, we all have internal lie detectors that we constantly use to determine if we believe what someone else is saying. We listen to their voice, we watch their face and their body language, and we pick up on many other signals of which we are not consciously aware. Therefore, one of the most successful and effective techniques to use before you start trying to convince someone else is to use your own built-in "lie detector" on yourself. Set up your video camera and record yourself talking about why you believe you are correct in your position on the issue. Then carefully watch the video several times, as objectively as possible, focusing on different aspects of your presentation. Listen and watch your face for whether your eyes and your facial muscles match the words you're saying. Also, listen and focus on the tone and other characteristics of your voice to see if you sound congruent with the message. Then focus on your body to see whether your gestures, or lack of gestures or inappropriate gestures, are congruent. Make notes of the particular parts of the message where your body language doesn't look like you really believe what you are saying. Take those issues and analyze them to see if you can find what is bothering you or your subconscious about them.

The written word is often the least effective way to communicate ideas or issues to others. This is exactly why people on the Internet developed "emoticons" to help add emotional understanding to their written word. This is a common example of an emoticon: ;<). So if you are convincing and selling others on your position, it's best not to rely on the written word but to speak to them in person or at least by voice or finally by video tape if you cannot speak to them in person. If you want to sell your idea, use the written word as a last resort.

The second main point to taking charge is to develop a plan and commit to implementing it. There are probably many people who have ideas about action that needs to be taken on some particular issue. Of those, a much smaller number will overcome their doubts and issues in order to develop a belief that they could and should do something to help solve the problem. But even fewer will actually develop a plan and implement it with a commitment to follow it through to completion. Talk is cheap, and a lot of people never get past the talking stage of, "We ought to do something about that." Let me give you an example. About twenty-five years ago, my oldest son Andy was a baby. After working in poverty programs and seeing so many people who couldn't read and what it had done to their lives, I had become concerned about our schools and their ability to teach people to read. I began researching and found that new education theories for teaching reading had been implemented to replace the old system of phonics. This "new"—at that time—technique basically taught memorizing words, and it didn't seem to be working, based on the poor readers I'd seen. Because of my belief that the ability to read is critical for a child to succeed, I believed something needed to be done. I talked to the teachers and administrators and was told that they had Ph.D.s in education, that they knew what would be best for my children and that I did not have the credentials to know what to do. I could have been intimidated or played victim, but because of my strong belief in the value of reading, I decided I couldn't just hope and wait. I don't play victim well, and it was time to take charge. Since I couldn't get help from the system, I found that I would have to do the teaching myself.

Andy liked to play with locks and keys, so I took that interest and explained that words were like locks. I developed a reading game that I called "locks and keys." He had always loved to have us read to him, and I explained that if he learned the sounds that letters made, they were like keys and he could learn how to unlock the words by himself. Using a puppet, with Cheetos® as a prize—amazingly both Andy and the puppet liked Cheetos®—Andy enjoyed learning the letters and the sounds they could make. He would get a chance to sound out a word. If he didn't get it, then the puppet would get a chance to sound it out and figure out what the word was. It turned out the puppet was very good at sounding out words that Andy hadn't figured out. Plus the puppet's techniques for unlocking the words helped reinforce for Andy the techniques that I had taught him. The puppet also loved Cheetos® and would exclaim loudly when he got a Cheeto®, which I palmed but pretended to feed to the puppet. The puppet would then chew and say, "Ooh" and "Ahh" as he chewed. Then the puppet would swallow and open his mouth and the Cheeto® would be gone. This puzzled Andy, as the puppet's throat was sewn closed. So the puzzlement of how the puppet ate the Cheeto® added a bit of magic to the fun. As a result, Andy learned to read when he was three years old and was reading at about the 9th grade level when he was five years old.

Because of my value on reading, I felt action had to be taken to make sure my children learned to read. I could have played victim and said that I would just leave it up to the school system, but I couldn't take that chance. I believed this was a serious issue. I developed a plan and made a commitment to teach them to read because I believed I could. I took charge and solved the problem by teaching both of my sons to read.

Wright

You've written that vision is one of the most important organizational responsibilities of a leader. How does a leader go about developing a vision for an organization?

Garner

The best leaders usually don't develop the vision by themselves. Instead they practice MBWA—Management By Wandering Around—and other techniques to get input and feedback from internal staff and external customers. These leaders and managers go out on the floor and visit with staff frequently and ask questions not only about how the staff is doing but also about ideas the staff has on how to improve their jobs. They encourage staff to think and to be creative in their tasks. These leaders convey that they value the staff's ideas and they also give staff the credit for ideas that work. They find out about issues that are bothering staff, and they ask them for their input on solutions. So they have their hand on the pulse of the company's morale. Again, because of the psychological penchant of our psyches to resist change, they encourage people to suspend disbelief and try to ask themselves about their jobs and how they could be better in the future. The "what if" question can be asked about many different things such as, "What thoughts have you had where you wondered, 'What if...?'" "Was it about quality or production or customer service?" "Tell me more about your idea." "If you were the boss, what would you do to better serve our customers or to make a better product?" Or "What do you think we'll be doing in twenty years?" I'm not suggesting you bombard someone with all these questions at once but rather that you use them as examples of open-ended questions to elicit thinking.

The best leaders are those who not only encourage creativity but also *listen* to staff, to customers, and also read about future prognostications. In so doing, they begin to develop ideas and get feedback from others about what the organization could or should do in the future. Those ideas are used to develop a new vision and to constantly refine the existing vision. Another excellent technique to trigger creative thinking is for leaders to ask questions in terms of "feelings." For example, a leader might ask such a question this way: "If you could make things different in the future, what would it look like? What would it feel like? What would it sound like? How would customers feel about it?" By encouraging staff to involve their senses, the leader triggers more whole-brain thinking and thereby more comprehensive ideas about improvements. It can actually trigger someone to visualize the future as if he were describing a movie he's watching, as his brain operates in ways that are difficult to express. Part of the reason for that is that people think, listen and understand differently. If you involve the senses, somebody might get more involved in actually being part of the creative process and thinking about the particular way he actually processes information.

In keeping with the idea that a good leader is asking for input and ideas, it is critical for a leader to keep track of where good ideas come from and to recognize staff members for those ideas. This is important for several reasons. First, recognition is generally a bigger motivator than money, except for low-paid staff. When a leader gives credit for an idea to a particular staff person, it not only clearly says that this staff member made a major contribution, but it also sends out a powerful message to other staff members that they will also be given credit for their ideas if they help the organization. A second, subtler, message is that the leader is not so egotistical that he or she has to try to get credit for everything to help build his or her self at the expense of the staff. A third benefit of giving credit to a staff member goes back to the issue of change management and the general resistance of people to change. In many organizations, staff members at lower levels often feel that top management may be so far removed from the actual work that they don't realize the implications of changes that they are trying to implement. However, the leader might say something like this: "Bill Jones in the machine shop came up with a brilliant new idea that will save this organization $500,000 a year. Bill's idea has been analyzed and reviewed with others in other shops, and he is absolutely right. Therefore, we want to begin implementing Bill's idea." Employees affected by the proposed change, the shop workers, will respond better because it came from Bill Jones, and he knows exactly what happens in his shop and probably in similar shops, so his credibility is high.

The second part of the message is that management analyzed this and got input from others who work in that area and, perhaps, other machine shops. Bill Jones now becomes a part of company folklore. Let me point out that in this example, if Bill proposed a solution that will save $500,000 per year, while recognition by itself is great, this is not an insignificant sum, and Bill Jones should be rewarded with some type of monetary bonus. This incident will also go down in company folklore as a clear example of the leader demonstrating that he gives credit where credit is due and that rewards are commensurate with the benefits to the organization.

Wright

You've written about values and the relationship to organizational culture. How does a leader influence the culture, and why is it important in taking charge?

Garner

I believe that values are so important that they actually become the boss when the boss is not around. You may not realize it, but just as anthropologists go into jungles or deserts and describe cultures of different groups, anthropologists could go into most organizations that have been around for a while and describe their culture. In fact, the rumor mill is often a way of studying the values and folklore in an organization.

Anthropologists generally define culture as a set of shared beliefs, values, customs, behaviors and methods that members of the group use to cope with their world and with each other and that are passed down from one generation to the next. Good leaders realize that they have a role in either establishing, reinforcing or in changing unacceptable elements of the organizational culture. For example, a new manager takes over and through MBWA and other techniques finds that the previous manager was viewed as an egotistical maniac who took credit for everybody's ideas but made sure that blame was always hung around the neck of some unlucky subordinate. As a result, morale is lower than a snake's belly in a wagon rut and risk taking and creativity have completely disappeared. It becomes critical for the new manager to make sure he encourages creativity and risk taking and then absolutely gives credit to staff members for their ideas.

We have recently seen national examples of leaders who have adversely affected their companies' organization. Enron demonstrates how top managers became greedy and used shell games to shuffle profits and expenses. Then when people began to ask how their accounting firm, Arthur Andersen, could have missed these accounting shell games, the truth came out that the consulting division of Arthur Andersen had apparently approved plans and then applied pressure to the accounting division to cover up the shell games. A key value of an accounting firm has to be professional integrity and honesty in objectively auditing a company's books. That value was apparently compromised in Arthur Andersen and, as a result, that company died along with Enron. A key point to note here is that an organization's culture can vary significantly from what that organization states as its written values. For example, a company might say that it always deals honestly with its customers. Then a new employee in the accounting department finds that a customer has overpaid on an order by several thousand dollars and points this out to the boss. The boss replies, "Make a note of it in the file, but let's just wait and see if they catch it. If they don't, it will just be extra profit for us." The new employee now knows that the company's values are significantly different than what he just read about in the company material in the new employee orientation. He also may realize that he will have to very carefully check his pay stubs, because if the company will cheat its external customers, then it will probably cheat its internal customers, staff members. Also the new employee doesn't have to find out if higher level management supports this idea of cheating customers, because to him, his boss represents management and the company. Finally, if this employee ever finds that the company has accidentally overpaid him, he may feel that it will be up to the company to find the error and that he is under no obligation to say anything since that's the way the company treats others.

On the positive side, a leader's actions are often much more important than the words they've published in personnel handbooks or mission statements. An example that I will remember the rest of my life was the state of fear that existed in our country after the September 11, 2001, terrorist bombings. The president had urged Americans to go about their business and not to succumb to the fears created by the terrorists or they would have accomplished what they intended to do by crippling our country. Then when we heard that the president was going to throw out the first ball to open the baseball season, there was a sense of heightened fear, as he would be so exposed to possible threats. I sat on the edge of my seat, held my breath and watched along with millions of others as President Bush walked out to the pitcher's mound, stopped and calmly threw a strike into the glove of the catcher. More than anything he could have said, his actions demonstrated that he felt we should not be cowering in our homes but that we should have the courage to go out and get on with our lives. Plus, by throwing a strike, he demonstrated he was able to focus on the moment, under pressure, and do the job well.

Another key way a leader influences the culture is to hire the right people, train them and then delegate to them the authority to do their jobs. Many managers will hire, train and then micromanage. If you don't think this can be a serious problem, consider that analysis shows that one of the basic problems with the Vietnam War was that it was micromanaged by President Johnson and by management "guru" Robert McNamara, who should have known better. The American military was hog-tied with limitations and not given clear goals and objectives or the authority to prosecute the war. Then direct orders were shipped out of the White House for specific targets in Vietnam, based on information that was days old and out of date. Troops were asked to capture specific pieces of ground at great cost, then to retreat, because there were no clear goals and objectives of what was to be accomplished.

If you and your organization can't come up with clear goals and objectives and delegate to well-trained staff, then it won't help you to micromanage in hopes that no one will notice. Hire, train and delegate with appropriate authority to meet known goals and objectives within a good set of organizational values and you will create a culture conducive to success. The next time you have an urge to micromanage well-trained, qualified staff, remember what micromanagement, the lack of clear goals and objectives, and failure to delegate did during the Vietnam War. Delegate before you stir up a protest movement that may force you to withdraw.

Wright

As a professional speaker and speech coach, what techniques do you recommend for leaders in developing skills to communicate their vision and values?

Garner

For years, conventional wisdom has been that business communications should be short, certainly no more than one page, with simple words and few adjectives. It would appear that there was no effort to teach business people how to speak, as so many business people feel that if they have to give a speech, it should be done by reading a very short, dry page of numbers and facts and then sit down. I have listened to business people speak who could have been trained in hypnotism techniques, as their monotone delivery and boring recitations of facts made my eyelids become heavy in a few short minutes. Several times I have had to fight to stay in the chair and not slide right onto the floor. Trying to focus on what they were saying only heightened the hypnotic effect. I even heard one top executive walk up to the podium and say, "I'm not a very good speaker, so I'm going to read my speech." Afterwards, people expressed how boring that was and how it would have been better if he had just handed out copies to everyone and sat down. Having to listen to someone give a pitiful delivery of poorly written material is negatively motivating. Staff members are often ashamed of such managers and might not even be willing to follow them to the bar for free drinks.

Abraham Lincoln was a master storyteller who used that technique to make his points. He seemed to have an endless supply of stories to illustrate almost any point, and people loved to get him in small groups and hear him tell stories. He read constantly and sought stories from his visits and travels. But in addition to his skills at personal and public speaking, Lincoln was a masterful writer. His Gettysburg speech is one of the most famous speeches of all time, and yet most of us have only read it. We certainly never heard Abraham Lincoln deliver it. In fact, when Lincoln gave that short speech at the Gettysburg, Pennsylvania, battlefield, the speech was so short that the crowd did not realize he had finished for a little while after he stopped talking. Lincoln proved that great speeches don't have to be long to be effective and memorable. Lincoln clearly is known as one of our most famous presidents because of his values, his determination and his communication skills.

One common element of great communicators is that they feel passion for their subjects, and that passion comes across in their speeches. While Lincoln did not yell and bluster in giving his Gettysburg speech, no one can deny the strong emotions the speech stirs with its powerful words. Passion for a subject can be a very strong tool and can be abused. In fact, there have been infamous speakers who used passion to stir up throngs of people to do terrible deeds. But it makes the point in a negative way that passion can get people to listen to your speech and to act on it. As a further note, I would suggest that people who are asked to give speeches about subjects that they do not feel strongly about are not likely to be effective unless they are very good actors. Dale Carnegie taught thousands of people how to speak in public, and he emphasized as a basic point that they should speak about things that they know well and in which they believe.

Use personal stories instead of someone else's stories. If you tell your own story, it will flow naturally and with sufficient detail to capture the audience. Telling other people's stories makes it appear that you don't have enough experience to have your own stories. Stories don't have to be funny. They can simply be told as a short story. For example, the manager in our earlier example could say something like, "The other day, I was down in the machine shop talking to staff members about their ideas on how we can improve our company. Bill Jones, one of our top mechanics, showed me some of our production equipment and told me about an idea he had to improve production and quality at the same time. We have talked to other people about Bill's idea, and after further research, it looks like Bill's idea will save the company about $500,000 per year. Bill, stand up so those people who don't know you can see one of our company's heroes!" The manager could have simply announced a new program that will save $500,000 if he was from the old ineffective school of communication. But by telling this short story, he reinforces that he does MBWA, that he encourages people to be creative and that he listens and gives credit to people who have ideas and do good work. He reinforces company folklore about himself as to how he demonstrates values, not just talks about them. And he put Bill's name into the company folklore as a hero.

A third simple technique is the one mentioned earlier. Review your body language by videotaping your presentation and reviewing it yourself. Unfortunately, many people are more afraid of speaking to a camera and then watching themselves than they are of just speaking to an audience. It can be painful to watch yourself practicing a speech, but when you do, you will notice things that you might otherwise have only found out if you had hired a speech coach. Most of your subordinates will simply not have the courage to give you the kind of feedback you need to improve your speaking skills.

Finally, I want to emphasize a key point for a leader to remember when he is considering writing a memorandum or giving a speech on an issue that is of concern to him. As we have noted earlier, staff members tend to watch what the leader does and what he says. But for some psychological reason, staff members also tend to think that the subject of the current memo or speech is more important than the subject of last year's speech or memo. Over the years, I've seen leaders become concerned about some particular aspect of the business and decide that they need to reinforce this point or value such as customer service, quality of the product, timeliness or some other aspect of the business. By speaking only on a single subject, the leader often creates what I call a "pendulum effect" in the business. Staff members listen and begin to put emphasis on this particular aspect at the expense of the other core values of the business. I believe one of the key jobs of the leader is to help reinforce the difficult job staff members have of maintaining a *balance* in quality, customer service, timeliness and business costs. If, for example, the boss sends out a letter or gives a speech saying that costs are too high and he wants them reduced immediately, staff may get the idea that reducing costs is now more important than quality, customer service or the timeliness of delivery. This is not necessarily a passive-aggressive response, as one might at first think, but rather it seems to be a part of our psyche to think that if that's all the boss is talking about, then that must be the most important thing he wants or he would have mentioned the other values. Consequently, someone, for example, might take the initiative to reduce costs by cutting back on quality control to get more product out the door. Then someone in shipping might decide to select a slower delivery method to save shipping costs. The results would be that the boss's stated goal in his last speech is met, and the company saves money, but the pendulum will swing over to the need to deal with all the customer complaints about poor quality and slow delivery. Therefore, let me emphasize that what the boss says in writing or in a speech needs to always reinforce the values and importance of meeting all the goals of the organization. Particularly, the leader must emphasize maintaining a *balance* in quality, customer service, costs and timeliness. Keeping these techniques in mind will help ensure that not only do staff members listen to you but that the outcomes of your speech or memo are the correct ones.

Wright

You've spent over twenty-four years researching and teaching creativity and how to develop abilities to become more creative. You've written that the best organizations are the ones that encourage creativity. Can a leader fan the spark of creativity and still focus on achieving goals and objectives?

Garner

In great organizations, the staff is encouraged to think and to provide feedback, and the managers and leaders to listen. If you believe that leaders should listen to staff members and create their visions from staff input, then you have to hire intelligent staff members and expect them to think about the future and how to make it better for them and for the organization. You need to set up ways for people to provide input, plus you need to do the MBWA to personally reinforce and encourage people to talk to management. Provide recognition and rewards that reinforce and publicize the contributions of staff. Some sophisticated and creative companies actually allow staff to take a certain percentage of their time or, with special approval, to participate in skunk works where staff members get together on their own initiative and brainstorm issues that concern them, to try to develop ideas and solutions.

The leader or manager can use the simple technique discussed earlier of asking "What if?" to encourage staff members to think about what the future might be like under different scenarios. Another powerful tool a manager may use to encourage thinking is to use the "5 Why" tool. You can use this technique when MBWA, during brainstorming sessions or when reviewing proposals. If a manager asks why something is done a certain way, the first response will usually be, "Because that's the way we've always done it." If the leader then says, "Yes, but why?" he will encourage the person to try and think back a little and, perhaps, a little deeper. The next response may often be some level of rationalization or reason that has been passed down. The bottom line is that the basis of the "5 Why" rule is that you often have to ask "Why?" five times to get to the real truth or understanding of why something is being done. Be advised that this tool can seem very frustrating at first, because we often don't like to have to think too deeply about why we are doing things. After a while, however, people will begin to understand that you want them to think and analyze, and they will begin looking at things more deeply, because they know you want them to think. The result of this deeper thinking is that when they begin to incorporate this into everyday life, they become more creative, because they begin questioning why things are done the way they are and whether they could be done differently.

Wright

After all these ideas about how to take charge, what do you think is the characteristic that has made more leaders successful?

Garner

Taking charge is critical, as are all the points we've mentioned that will help someone take charge and be successful. But on major projects and difficult tasks, there are often many naysayers, who constantly look for, and share with you, all the reasons you can't succeed and will fail. Due to the psychological requirements of the grieving process we all go through whenever we make a major change, even a positive change, there is an additional requirement that separates the good starters from the long-distance runners that make it across the finish line. That quality is perseverance, or some might call it dedication or discipline. Thomas Edison expressed this in the memorable statement that his work was, "one percent inspiration and ninety-nine percent perspiration." After Edison had the idea of inventing a light bulb, he made more than 1,200 attempts to get a filament before finally succeeding. Another man with the same idea but without the perseverance might have quit. In fact, in many companies, Edison might have been told to go on to another project.

This characteristic of perseverance could be one of the major defining characteristics of a champion. Throughout history, we see time after time where success occurred because there was a champion who believed and wouldn't quit. I felt like I was in good company when I was accused of being "like a bulldog" when it comes to projects. Often that dedication to my beliefs and perseverance was all that kept me going when the going got difficult and everyone was saying it couldn't be done. I believed in my staff members and myself, and we stuck to it. As another example, I've heard some managers say that they like to hire college graduates because of the simple fact that the college graduate has proven that he can stick to a difficult multi-year job and see it through to completion.

Being willing to take charge of a major task is just the beginning. Make sure you're committed to the long haul and hang in there. You'll also find that the adage that "success breeds success" is absolutely true. The more you succeed, the easier it is to persevere on the next project. One idea I had for an improvement literally took ten years to implement, because there was so much resistance. But the perseverance paid off, and the results benefited hundreds of thousands of people. I believe perseverance and dedication are keys to achieving success. If you're ready to become a champion for some issue or task, take charge and persevere! You, too, can make a difference!

Wright

Gary, I really appreciate the time you have allotted today for this interview for *Taking Charge*. On the note of persistence, which is a good one to stop on, I want to tell you how much I appreciate you taking this time.

Garner

Thank you.

Wright

Today we have been talking to Gary Garner, who is a professional speaker and consultant. Thank you very much.

Gary A. Garner
Garner Consulting and Communication
2204 Bonita
Austin, Texas 78703
Phone: 512.689.4778
Fax: 512.474.9942
Email: gary@garygarner.com
www.garygarner.com

Chapter 3

DON SCHMINCKE

Don Schmincke is the author of The Code of the Executive *and has been featured by CNN,* The Wall Street Journal *and* USA Today. *From MIT and Johns Hopkins, Don uses anthropology and genetics to show why many leadership programs fail, and he offers astonishing alternatives to dispel "program-of-the-month" theories. Current projects include books on tribal leadership and bioevolutionary relationships. Occasionally, Don can be found at MBA programs, wreaking havoc on leadership theories and inflicting his unconventional techniques on innocent graduate students.*

David E. Wright (Wright)

As author of the underground best seller, *The Code of the Executive,* Mr. Schmincke's unusual and groundbreaking work has been endorsed by Stephen Covey and Brian Tracy and featured by CNN, *The Wall Street Journal* and other national media. A graduate of MIT and Johns Hopkins University, Don's controversial and provocative approach uses anthropology and genetic evolutionary science to show why many leadership, strategy and change programs fail, and it offers unique and astonishing alternatives to dispel "program-of-the-month" theories. He has toured U.S. military operations by invitation of the secretary of defense—he is still recovering from being shot off an aircraft carrier—and has traveled extensively throughout the world, including the former Soviet Bloc, Africa and Asia, in order to research this topic. Occasionally, Don can be found at MBA programs wreaking havoc on leadership theories and inflicting his unconventional techniques on innocent graduate students. Don, it is really great to have you with us today.

Don Schmincke (Schmincke)

Thanks for having me.

Wright

I was interested in one of your workshops based on your book *The Code of the Executive*. You state that most executives are frustrated with the level of results produced by the organizations or the politics, hidden agendas and other dysfunctional behaviors sapping organizational vitality. Could you name some of these behaviors?

Schmincke

Sure. We see these behaviors often as we work with hundreds of executives each year to take their strategy or leadership to the next level. Typically, we find that what is stopping their organization's performance are patterns of behavior that look like territoriality, blaming, CYA, looking good to the boss, finger pointing, withholding information, back stabbing, accountability avoidance, taking credit for another's ideas and numerous other selfish behaviors for power and control. What's interesting is that these behaviors are usually accepted as normal, but everyone thinks no one else notices. People think that their hidden agendas are really hidden. Our executive retreats give us an opportunity to research and learn how ancient methods address these issues as well as help companies eradicate these leadership hemorrhages.

Wright

As I was listening to you, I was wondering if one could take corporation out of the equation and put family in there. It sounded like my family.

Schmincke

It is interesting that you say that, because most of our work is with human groups, and so many tell us it really does transfer to families. In fact, my partner Charlie Davis got a call from a couple of little girls who just wanted to thank him for "giving us our daddy back." Apparently, their father was a participant at one of our retreat experiences. Our approach is designed to produce breakthroughs in human organizations, so I guess families, soccer teams, political parties or religious groups are organizations, too, and can benefit. From my recent research of evolutionary genetics, I am convinced these behaviors occur within humans naturally because of instinctive patterns wired into our DNA. Any human group of strangers from various cultures will quickly begin to exhibit these behaviors, so the existence of these behaviors probably enhanced our ability to replicate and survive as a species. The problem today is that there are new phenomena occurring in civilization. Now we have to figure out how to work and lead, given these ancient designs in our bodies.

Wright

I remember talking to Larry Wilson several years ago. One of his favorite anthropologists was a fellow named Ashley Montague. I think he was just in love with the name. It's such a great name. How does anthropology relate to what you're doing?

Schmincke

Some years ago, I was winning awards for the work I was doing with Fortune-level CEOs and their executives, but then the scientist in me took over, and I started doing research on the results of modern management theory and was stunned by the high failure rates. For example, Michael Beer's research at Harvard showed an inability to trace bottom-line results from any large-scale change program. Other studies showed failure rates of change programs, quality programs and teams to be from fifty to eighty percent. I was shocked but more so by the fact that no one was talking about it! Why were executives still buying a lot of books from management gurus? Why were these failure rates not mentioned in the consulting brochures? And what are we missing that does work, because there have been successful organizations for thousands of years? So I chose the only science that I thought could answer that question—anthropology. Luckily, my background isn't in business; it is in science. So I was able to integrate this approach into our work. One thing led to another, and I became this author of alternative leadership approaches based on a scientific viewpoint.

Wright

In the same workshop that I referred to before, on your book *The Code of the Executive,* you take your attendees on a journey into ancient history to rediscover lost insights that have propelled organizations to success for thousands of years. Could you give us an overview of these insights?

Schmincke

Yes. It has been fascinating taking the scientific approach, because many organizations, including some well-known leadership organizations, have chosen us to help them because of these unique insights. I think they are jaded by the modern management hype and leadership fashion trends. The approach of using controversial ancient insights offers a refreshing alternative. You see, we find that many managers get seduced by just altering the processes or the content of their companies instead of realizing that there is something deeper than that. This seduction causes us to spend billions of dollars in change programs with life cycles of only three to five years. I am faced with this thorny question when I teach at MBA programs: How do I tell the students that by the time they graduate, most of what they will learn will probably be wrong? Will they notice that when they graduate, there will be a whole new set of best selling books on how to run their companies better? Has anyone noticed that we spend millions of dollars in leadership training and all we end up with is *Dilbert*™? These are all clues that there are deeper questions, and I think if we explore these questions, we'll realize that there is nothing bad about process or structural changes and that what seems to be missing is that human behavior fails to shift from these changes. When a change program is introduced into an organization, it could be world class, but if human behavior fails to change, then the program will ultimately fail. But if we go deeper, we discover an interesting insight: People only behave according to what they believe in. If we wish to change organizations, we must change their beliefs. I have found that using anthropology and evolutionary genetics reveals that most leadership and management theories fail because people's beliefs fail to change. What we found works best are the methods to alter beliefs, but most MBA graduates and managers today have no training in belief management.

There is another insight we discovered from analyzing the Samurai, a topic of my earlier book, *The Code of the Executive*, and a training program for managers written seven hundred years ago. It pertains to the military fact that speed wins. Faster armies out-maneuver slower armies. It also pertains to the corporate fact that faster companies out-maneuver slower companies. Faster companies have higher market share penetration rates and higher profitability. But if we look at what causes organizations to slow down, it's precisely the behaviors we already talked about—the territoriality, the CYA, the blaming, the looking good to the boss, the finger pointing—all of that stuff. Our research shows that an average of fifty percent of human capital is wasted in organizations from these dysfunctional behaviors. Get rid of them and you get speed. That is a key leadership issue, but shockingly, eradicating these behaviors in order to regain fifty percent of lost human capital is a goal that is consistently missing on the priority lists of many companies. You would think it would be one of the top three strategic priorities, but we never find it mentioned.

The controversial insight we learned from ancient executives is that the source of these dysfunctional behaviors is the *ego*. The samurai didn't have the term ego, so they called it "the evil spirit of the executive," which I think is a much more accurate description. It is the ego that makes dysfunctional behavior righteous and appropriate in the world in which employees believe they exist. This is an amazing insight. Most programs avoid or paint over these behaviors as if they are there because of some lack of training. We approach it totally differently. These behaviors are there because they are "correct" behaviors in the reality the employees perceive! People don't behave in a dysfunctional manner because they think they are wrong but because they think they are right. Until you alter their beliefs about their reality, they won't go away. But how do you unhook the ego and increase speed? This method is not taught in business schools, yet we are trying to change that, even though it is controversial. But to ancient executives it was obvious—death. This provocative, but effective, insight, I think, has been lost to history and allowed fertile ground for *Dilbert*™ to be born. The problem today is that executives don't know how to die or, in other words, how to subjugate their ego to a higher cause. Suicide of the ego and older beliefs are important if new beliefs are to be born. Ancient executives knew that through death you can free the ego, and that's why the first sentence in the book was that the executive must keep in mind constantly by day and by night the fact that someday he must die. We teach death for the freedom and power it offers leaders and to diminish *Dilbert*™-like leadership in an organization.

Executives see this freedom made available by death happen all the time. When they fire someone, all of a sudden, that employee starts telling the truth. When a company nears bankruptcy, all of a sudden, it begins making different decisions. Why is this? Because they're already dead! But wouldn't it be great if you had an organization where people would tell the truth while they were still employed and make great decisions before bankruptcy?

Wright

In another one of your workshops, you talk about the backlash against the consulting industry for not producing results after billions of dollars have been spent. You alluded to it just now. In addition, you state that managers are hesitant to pursue another program-of-the-month. What are some of the alternatives you teach them?

Schmincke

We see this a lot, because when we go into an organization, we sometimes get warned about the organization's cynicism from bad experiences with previous consultants or the frustration with the last change program that never really resulted in anything. What do we do? As you can tell by now, we encourage a different approach. For instance, we seek truth, not seduction; seek beliefs, not structures or processes. A lot of management theory is seductive, because it is very logical, linear and predictable. But leading from belief is somewhat illogical, somewhat irrational and emotional. However, leading from beliefs works! It has for thousands of years. Our alternatives are to ask deeper questions, unhook "evil," seek truth, abandon pop business culture, expose the real issues versus painting over them and rely on the lasting wisdom available from anthropology, poetry, physics, your children and yourself. Those are the areas where insights are more meaningful.

Wright

The wideness of knowledge makes a person better rounded and allows special learning to take place, right?

Schmincke

Yes. But what I think is ironic is that many poor managers seek the narrow knowledge. They brag about all the books they are reading, but the books are from the same pool. There is little that is new. Salvation does not come from proficiency with buzzwords.

Wright

Right. I remember that when transactional analysis came out in the seventies or eighties, I read every book. I was turned into an armchair psychologist there for a few minutes. I would agree with the stretching out into different areas and going outside the box. I did hear a great educator one time many years ago say that if you graduated from college and earned a

B.S. or a B.A. degree five years ago and you haven't kept reading or gone to seminars or workshops or self-educated yourself, you are uneducated again.

Schmincke

You know, if we ask deeper questions, we'll find things that have actually worked for thousands of years. I think those are much more interesting. The problem is that they are not usually talked about that much.

Wright

What do you tell managers and leaders who are uncertain that their current team is sufficient to win tomorrow's challenges?

Schmincke

A couple of things. If their current team is weak and incapable, then I guess I wouldn't tell them anything. I would ask them a few questions like, "Why are they there? Who hired them? How did this team come to be?" If the team has been weakened and has been in the organization for a long time, it may be symptomatic of a deeper problem. Somebody had to hire these people, and somebody had to put them together in the configuration they are in. What is that all about?

Wright

How do you view team building? In other words, are teams better off with a mixture of personality styles, or is it best to start out with like-minded people whose personalities are similar?

Schmincke

Statistics show that most teams fail. I don't think it's due to a choice of personalities, because people don't have to like each other or even be polite, but they do need integrity, honor and bravery. But when was the last time you saw team training on honor and bravery? I think having a profile of the different strengths necessary to produce the result is good. I think it is not the personalities but the beliefs that need to be shared and aligned. More deeply than that, those people need to have a certain level of integrity, honor and bravery in order to align their beliefs with each other so that they can become powerful. It takes a lot more than just standard platform-training programs.

Wright

You really do believe in going back to the basics, don't you?

Schmincke

Definitely. And it works. I think we are the only management-consulting group in the United States that has a money-back guarantee on our results. The only reason we can do that is we use stuff that has been proven to work for thousands of years.

Wright

With our talk show and book, we are trying to encourage people in our audience and our readers to be better and to live better and be more fulfilled by listening to the examples of our guests. Is their anything or anyone in your life that has made a difference for you and helped you to become a better person?

Schmincke

My wife has helped me become a better father. My mother has helped me become a better son. As a POW, my father taught me bravery.

The "things" that have made a difference for me are the existential and ontological philosophies, particularly the study of the dimensions of suffering and enlightenment in the Buddhist and early Christian works. These philosophies help me come back to the world in a different way.

Wright

How would the study of suffering relate to something that might be wrong in a corporation? Or does it?

Schmincke

Well, if something's wrong in a corporation, somebody is probably suffering.

Wright

Right. Either financially—

Schmincke

Either financially or the stockholders or somebody's project or territory or career. So yes, suffering can be found a lot in corporations, especially in leadership, because we find that a lot of leaders end up doing stupid things and exhibiting selfish behavior. They have not learned to detach from their fears, detach from their suffering. They have let their ego run the agenda, and they are going to put the company and the customer in second place to their selfish agendas. This all plays out in every *Dilbert*™ comic we see, so it is very typical of human behavior and has been for thousands of years. Go back and read any ancient document and you will see CEOs and executive teams trying to get something done but running into the whole political quagmire. It's part of our humanity. I think the issue of freedom and death and detachment is much more relevant in management training than anything I've researched, but I'm just consistently shocked why it's never taught and never used by management consultants.

Wright

I remember several years ago, I wrote a program on leadership for a national real estate chain, and I found myself quoting Peter Drucker and Warren Bennis a lot, and I started reading both and even talking to Bennis. I found that they were like you; they were into going back to the basics and getting to the deeper meanings of the deeper truths. I almost, without their knowledge, think of them as mentors. What do you think makes up a great mentor? In other words, are there characteristics that mentors seem to have in common?

Schmincke

I think three characteristics come to mind. One I mentioned is detachment, the ability to be there but not be consumed or seduced by the journey of the person you are mentoring—almost a non-judgementalness. I don't mean avoiding judging what's right and wrong, but detaching so that you can be present to where they are. Secondly, I think a mentor needs to be able to see further and deeper than his protégé. Sometimes that's hard to find in a mentor. Third, I think he should have a way of holding his protégé accountable. There needs to be some accountability support.

Wright

Most people are fascinated with these new television shows about being a survivor. There's one popping up every day. What has been the greatest comeback you have made from adversity in your career or in your life for that matter?

Schmincke

I can't think of any great comeback, but I can think of a lot of small ones. Throughout my life, there have been a lot of small adversities, but whenever a prized opportunity, desire, program or whatever I was working on got shut down or bogged down, I always found it was a message that that was really not the path. As soon as I accepted that, an even greater destiny always emerged. As I have gotten older, I now see that when I get blocked, there's another way. And it's always much better.

Wright

So the little hills we have to climb over probably build our character and teach us the real truths more than anything else, in the final analysis.

Schmincke

Yes. I think so. I think it's an everyday experience, at least for me.

Wright

Well, I've never lost an arm or a leg or gotten caught in a fire or doing a lot of things like some speakers that I talk to on a daily basis. They have these great stories about something that was really catastrophic, but the everyday living is bad enough for me. Some lessons I've had to learn several times over again. It's almost as if I get tired of learning the same lesson. When you consider the choices you've made down the years, has faith played an important role in your life?

Schmincke

Yes, and it still does. I think the impossible and the invisible require faith. In my book the "death" issue really allowed me to look into myself and find the freedom and power that comes from having faith in those things. I think my struggle over the years has been to try to incorporate that into corporate work as well. For example, right now, we have a handful of committed people who take clients on journeys that we have where faith will make a difference. We have so much faith we even put our money where our mouth is and guarantee it. We are very clear that whether we get called to help a company take its strategy to a new level or its executive leadership to a new level, we have to have faith that these ancient designs will produce those results, or we give the money back.

Wright

I remember reading Helen Kubler-Ross's book *On Death and Dying* many, many years ago. It helped me tremendously in understanding and settling some questions I had, until I got to the point where one of my friends committed suicide. I tried to understand that by reading everything I could find on the subject of suicide for two years, only to learn at the end of the second year that I didn't know anything more than what I did when I began. It's a very difficult subject.

Schmincke

It is very difficult, and it can be a very painful subject. But what we find metaphorically in organizations is that people get power if they can learn to commit suicide to those parts of themselves that stop them from being great. It's interesting that you mention that, because a lot of times people say, "I want to change my organization or my department," and we come in and seek what has to die first. What do you have to kill? Old beliefs will stop any change program. Suicide is painful when you try to kill the ego or beliefs that want to stay alive. It's a very difficult journey, but when you read the literature of great leaders throughout history, these are consistent themes.

Wright

If you could have a platform and tell our audience and our readers something that you feel would help or encourage them, what would you say to them?

Schmincke

I would say that whenever you face a challenge that you find to be insurmountable or that causes some level of suffering, the first thing to do is just stop. Because a lot of times what's happening is we are getting attached to something, and until we can just stop and take a breath and look at it fresh, there is no hope. The second thing is to ask better questions. We are so inundated with answers today. I mean, we have the Web throwing answers at us, and we've got 30,000 business books a year on leadership being thrown at us. We've got too many answers. I think we need to start asking better questions. Thirdly, I guess I would just say to love people anyway. In the end, we are all human. Love yourself, because you're going to make mistakes. People are going to be jerks and annoy us and get in the way, but that's all part of a journey. I think love has a place in business and leadership.

Wright

I really appreciate you being a guest today. It has been very interesting.

Schmincke

Thank you.

Wright

We have been talking today with Don Schmincke. He is the author of *The Code of the Executive*, an unusual, alternative view of leadership. He can be found speaking, writing, consulting or, as he says, wreaking havoc on innocent graduate students. Thank you so much, Don, for being with us today.

Schmincke

You're welcome.

Don Schmincke
1400 William St.
Baltimore, MD 21230
Phone: 410.528.0800
Email: Don@executivecode.com
www.sagaworldwide.com

Chapter 4

JIM KOUZES

Jim is a highly-regarded leadership scholar and experienced executive. The Wall Street Journal *has cited him as one of the twelve most requested non-university executive-education providers to U.S. companies. Jim is the Chairman Emeritus of Tom Peters Company, a professional service firm that specializes in developing leaders at all levels. He is also an Executive Fellow at the Center for Innovations and Entrepreneurship at Santa Clara University's Leavey School of Business.*

David E. Wright (Wright)

Today we are talking to Jim Kouzes, who, along with Barry Posner, is the co-author of the award-winning book, *The Leadership Challenge*, which has more than a million copies in print. It was first published in 1987, and the third edition was published in the fall of 2002. *The Leadership Challenge* is available in eleven languages and has been a selection of the McMillan Executive Book Club and the Fortune Book Club. It is the winner of the 1989 James A. Hamilton Hospital Administrator Book Award and the 1995-96 Critics' Choice Award.

Jim has also written several books with co-author Barry Credibility, including *How Leaders Gain and Lose It, Why People Demand It*, which was chosen by *Industry Week* as one of the ten best management books of 1993. Their recent books include *Encouraging the Heart* and *Leadership Challenge Planner*, released in 1999. In addition to their books, Jim and Barry have created The Leadership Practices Inventory, a 360-degree leadership assessment tool. Jim Kouzes, it is a pleasure to be with you today.

Jim Kouzes (Kouzes)

Thank you very much, David. It's my pleasure.

Wright

Tell us a little about your research for *The Leadership Challenge.* I read that you wanted to know what leaders did when they were at their personal best. How did you go about discovering that?

Kouzes

We were inspired by the Olympics. Having experienced the 2002 winter Olympics here in the United States, I think many of us can recall that a lot of athletes were talking about their personal best times and their personal best events. We got inspired by that concept and thought, "What if we asked leaders to tell us about their personal best performances? How will they talk about that? What would they identify? What would they say they did as leaders when performing at their best?" And, most importantly, would there be a pattern across stories, or would these cases be entirely idiosyncratic? We were intrigued by that and began a project to investigate leaders' personal best experiences. This took place at Santa Clara University, where I was director of the Executive Development Center at the time and Barry Posner was, and still is, a professor.

Our research began by asking leaders to tell us about their personal best leadership experiences—times when they functioned at their peak of performance. Interviews have been conducted with more than five hundred leaders. Approximately 7,500 leaders have written responses to the short-form Personal Best Leadership questionnaire, and about 4,000 have responded to the long-form questionnaire. So we have a lot of case data behind us that form the research.

A couple of years into our case collection, we developed an instrument we could use to survey individual leaders. This tool led to the development of The Leadership Practices Inventory (LPI). We have an extensive database—about 100,000 people are not included in it—but more than 300,000 leaders and 750,000 observers have actually completed the questionnaire. In addition, more than 175 doctoral dissertations and masters theses have been written using the LPI as the research tool. This makes our model one of the most extensively researched in the entire field. Well over a million people have been involved in the research on our model in one way or another.

Wright

A million people—that would almost be a zero margin of error, wouldn't it?

Kouzes

There will always be some margin of error. If anyone ever stood up in front of me and said he could determine with one hundred-percent accuracy why people do things, I think I would pack my bags and leave the seminar or turn off the radio, because there's no one factor, no one model that accounts for one hundred-percent human behavior. But we do know that our data are valid and reliable.

We made an important assumption from the beginning of our research that leadership was not about organizational level or position, and it's been supported over time. You don't have to turn to the CEOs of the world, you don't have to turn to the presidents of countries, and you don't have to turn to the high-profile politicians or the super athletes to learn about leadership. We asked people in the middle of different organizations—whether they were for-profit or non-profit companies, governmental agencies or community-based organizations—to tell us about their personal best.

We collected cases from young people—boys and girls as young as eight years old—who started organizations for youth to take on environmental causes or other kinds of issues in their communities. We talked to people in their seventies and eighties whose personal bests occurred late in their lives as well as in their middle years. We talked to people from many different countries. We talked to people in for-profit and non-profit companies, in government and in religious institutions. We talked to people from a variety of walks of life, and we found that people can identify at least one occasion in their lives when they think they did something at their personal best to move other people toward some shared vision, some shared purpose.

We found that you can learn as much from talking to those people—and probably more, in terms of what you and I can identify with—than by reading a biography about a CEO. There are only five hundred CEOs in the Fortune 500, but there are thousands and thousands of other leaders in those same Fortune 500 organizations. We like to describe the people we looked at as ordinary people who get extraordinary things done.

Wright

Did you find that these leaders had any problems defining their "personal best?"

Kouzes

All the people we asked were able to tell us about at least one time in their lives, in their careers, in their work, when they did something that they would consider their personal best.

Wright

That's fascinating. I was also fascinated by the fact that when you interviewed the people, you didn't stick to the obvious categories of planning, organizing, staffing, directing and controlling to get to personal leadership stories. How did you get stories of dynamic change and action?

Kouzes

We found out something very interesting, which continues to intrigue us. When you ask people to tell stories about their personal best experiences—and this applies whether you're talking to managers or employees—you find that people identify times of dramatic change. They recall times of turbulence or conflict or innovations. They talk about turning around an operation. They talk about starting up an operation. They talk about taking on a challenge that may have been extremely difficult. What people tend to do when they talk about their personal best is identify something that stretched them beyond what they thought their capacity was. So no, we didn't hear about ordinary projects that people worked on. We heard about things that were extraordinary from their perceptions. It's different from person to person, but more than eighty-five percent of the cases were about some kind of dynamic challenge, some adversity in their work lives or in their personal lives. There is a positive correlation between leadership and challenge and doing your best.

Wright

With the research that you did, were you able to refute the leadership stereotype? In other words, can almost anyone who desires to become a leader learn the behaviors necessary to succeed?

Kouzes

Based on our research, we would have to say yes. Everyone we asked had at least one story to tell about a time when they did their best. And if you display it once, it shows that you have the talent and the capacity and the ability to draw on those same resources again. Leadership is an observable set of skills and abilities. It's not some gene. Everyone has the potential to become a better leader than they are today. At the same time, our survey results tell us that some people do a better job at leading than others, and some individuals find it easier to do than others. But if you're asking if we can all learn to be better leaders than we are, the answer is an emphatic yes.

Wright

I had a great man help me tremendously early in my business career. I once worked for a large company, with many different offices, that just kept putting me in different jobs and moving me up higher and higher. I was in my late twenties and had the responsibilities of someone who should have been fifty or sixty. One day, I happened to tell this man that I was the leader, and he said, "No, you're not the leader. You're an awfully good manager. If you go outside and none of your employees follow you, then you're not a leader. You're just out for a walk." I didn't know what that meant at the time, but there are a lot of differences between leadership qualities and good managerial qualities, are there not?

Kouzes

All managers today have to be leaders, simply because of the nature of the work and the way it has changed in the context of work these days. Any organization that's going to really make a difference and differentiate itself in its industry or in the service it provides or in the young people it teaches is going to have to develop its managers as leaders, not just as people who do the typical kinds of planning, organizing, staffing, directing and controlling—the traditional definition of management. So in today's world, people are going to have to be both managers and leaders.

However, it's also true that leaders in other contexts, such as community activism or volunteering at a local school, don't necessarily have to be managers to be leaders. You can be a volunteer who comes in from the outside, or you can be a parent or a community member. You can be a church member and want to do something within an organization and to make some kind of significant contribution and lead a group of people. But you don't have to have a title. You don't have to be a manager. So there is a difference between what people do as managers and leaders. All managers must be leaders, but you don't have to be a manager to be a leader.

Wright

Lately, it seems that the people of the United States are demanding trust and credibility in their leaders, especially those at the top levels of businesses and the government. What do you think?

Kouzes

For more than twenty years, we've been researching the question, "What do you look for and admire in a leader, in someone whose direction you would willingly follow?" Note that the key word in that question is "willingly" follow, not "have to" follow; that is, you're conscripted, and this person is your boss, and you have to do what he says, but you willingly would choose to follow that person. Initially, we asked that as an opened-ended question. Later we developed a brief checklist of twenty items, each with several synonyms, and we asked respondents to select seven of the twenty. For more than twenty years, we've gotten a consistent set of responses. The same four descriptors have been selected by a significant majority of the people. The first is "honest"—chosen by eighty-eight percent of the people over twenty years. "Forward looking" is second on the list, with around seventy-one to seventy-five percent

Wright

Forward looking?

Kouzes

The ability to look beyond the current horizon of time and see ten, fifteen, twenty years ahead; to have a vision of the future; to be concerned about the future. The third quality is "competent," with sixty-six percent of the people selecting that, followed by "inspiring," with about sixty-five.

So to your point, "credibility" is one word that captures at least three of those descriptors—"honest," "competent" and "inspiring." And the one that differentiates leaders from other credible people is the quality of being forward looking—of having the capacity to look beyond the current horizon of time, of being concerned or optimistic about the future. If you had to sum up leadership in two words, I would say it is credibility plus vision.

Wright

Did you find that the forward-looking people were, for the most part, positive?

Kouzes

For a leader, the quality of being forward looking requires that he or she be optimistic about the future. You can't look out into the future and say, "Well, I'm pessimistic, and I think our country or our company or our division is going down the tubes. I'm not happy with the way the youth are today, and I'm not optimistic. I look at wars around the world, I look at the depletion of the oil reserves, and I look at nuclear proliferation. I look at all these things, and I predict a gloomy future." Those aren't the kinds of people we will willingly follow. We demand that a leader be optimistic and say, "You know, despite these problems we face—and they're all real problems that we can't ignore—I have confidence that we have the capacity to overcome them. We shall overcome."

If you listen to the speeches of great leaders, whether it's Martin Luther King or Winston Churchill or Mother Teresa or others who'd go on your list of your most admired historical leaders, you will find that optimism is one of their qualities. If you're Winston Churchill and London is being bombed on a daily basis, do you wake up in the morning saying, "We're doomed. We're going to give up." Or do you say, "This is happening to us, but we will overcome it. We will win. We will be victorious."

Wright

I was interested in your three-day The Leadership Challenge® Workshop, which is based on your book. I would think that a participant could learn a lot in three days, but the question is: In your experience, can change be affected in three days?

Kouzes

The Leadership Challenge® Workshop, whether it's the one-day, two-day or three-day version, can help people to learn knowledge and skill. We know from our own research and from others' that people can learn to improve their skills in a three-day period of time.

If I take a measure on day one and look at your skill at being forward-looking and then look at that again three days later, I know there's a measurable difference in what you could do on day one and what you can do on day three. However, as with any skill, there's the probability that you'll lose it if you don't practice it. So three days is a beginning, but it's not an end.

I learned to play golf when I was fifty-five years old. Just a couple of months ago, I went to play golf for three days. But I hadn't practiced in months, so it took me two days before I felt confident enough to hit the ball in a way that would get me around the course in under a hundred. Any skill gets lost if you don't practice it. You can go to a three-day course and learn some skills, but it's absolutely essential that you practice them on a regular basis.

One of the things we've found is that the best leaders are the best learners. They have an attitude of life-long learning. We've studied the relationship between learning and leadership and have found that those who score the highest in learning, regardless of their style of learning, have the highest scores as leaders and are the most effective leaders. They know that learning about leadership, or anything, is a life-long process and that they have to continuously engage in it.

We also know that the best leaders are those who ask for and listen to feedback from other people. They are the most self-aware people, and the most self-aware leaders are the most effective leaders. They ask for negative feedback, not just for affirming feedback for doing a good job. They want to know how they can improve, not just hear about how well they're doing.

Wright

Jim, I read that you grew up in Washington, D.C., and were one of the Boy Scouts selected to serve in John F. Kennedy's honor guard at his presidential inauguration. Inspired by that, you served two years as a Peace Corps volunteer. What was that experience like?

Kouzes

In 1960, after John F. Kennedy was elected, I was chosen as one of a dozen Eagle Scouts to serve in the honor guard at Kennedy's inauguration. If you can somehow get your hands on a January 1961 issue of *Life* magazine and find the photograph they took of us, I'm the third kid from the right. I look a little different today than I did back then. Imagine me being fifteen years old and in that position. My toes practically froze off my feet. It was so cold. I think it was nineteen degrees that day. It was just one of those memorable experiences, and I can still imagine myself being there today.

I look back on all those experiences—the opportunity to be on the White House lawn and to meet Kennedy up close; the chance to live and grow up in Washington, D.C., and to visit all the historical monuments; to be there when the Civil Rights movement was active and Martin Luther King was marching; to hear his speech over the radio as he was speaking at the Lincoln Memorial—all of those experiences caused me to be very interested in leadership.

I went to college to study political science, and then I vowed to my parents that I would join the Peace Corps after I graduated from college because I wanted to be part of it. I lived in another country, spoke another language, practiced different customs, worked, shopped and basically lived the life of a person who was native to that country. That, to me, was a life-changing experience.

If I could have a wish for every young person in this country, it would be to have a similar experience, because there's nothing that can teach a person more than an experience that is so different from one's daily life, such as having to live in a different country and speak a different language and live by different customs. What it taught me was respect and tolerance, openness to others and the knowledge that I could change the way I do things. I'm not stuck in a rut. I don't have to do things the same way. It gave me confidence that when faced with a challenge like that—learning another language, living in a different culture—I could meet that challenge. I think it helped me in the field I'm working in and has helped people who are attempting to make changes in their lives and in their careers and in their abilities to lead other people. It helped me in my work, but it also helped me understand that, when faced with adversity, I could overcome it and thrive on it and learn from it.

Wright

I'd like to turn our focus to how organizations thrive and survive. From my discussions with business leaders, there is almost a universal desire to grow and improve, but many leaders strike out before they're prepared, or they don't know what kind of help they need. How would you recommend organizations get the right kind of help before implementing any strategic initiative?

Kouzes

First, I think we need to reaffirm that our research clearly indicates that exemplary leaders are proactive. They seize the initiative to solve problems and take on challenges. Whenever you seize the initiative, as we know from our own experiences, the results can often be failures or mistakes or disasters. We find in our research with exemplary leaders that this in no way dampens their spirit to be proactive. So part of the answer to the question is to always accept that failure is a natural consequence of innovation and pro-activity and that it needs to be a learning experience.

On the other hand, leaders should also heed the advice of the late John Gardner, who served five presidents of the United States and was one of the preeminent writers on leadership. He said that we should "pity the leader caught between unloving critics and uncritical lovers." I love that quote. Leaders aren't always right, and because they are not always right, they need loving critics who can whisper in their ears, "I care about you, and on this one, you're off base. We need to take a step back and rethink this." So in addition to the best leaders being able to process their mistakes and step back and learn from them, they also are great takers of advice. They want to have honest feedback.

Finally, I'd say that the best leaders have great "outsight," not just great insight; that is, the ability to perceive external realities or the environment external to them. It's incumbent upon leaders to stay tuned to what's going on in the environment and not get caught by surprise. I'd ask three questions: What's happening in the external environment that surrounds my organization? What do I envision for this organization three to five years down the road? And what can I do to create a shared understanding of this image of the future? I would suggest those as places to start.

Wright

I've been guilty of diving into a new project, even with a decent plan, but never really being able to measure my progress or success. I imagine large organizations do the same thing. With this in mind, what would you advise companies to do as they move into the implementation stage of their plans?

Kouzes

There is some intriguing research by Albert Bandura at Stanford University that I think gives us some good hints about this. He found in his studies that people who set goals are no more motivated to improve their performances than people who don't set goals. He also found that when people receive only feedback, in the absence of goals, they're no more motivated than people who don't get feedback. Neither goals by themselves nor feedback on the progress you're making affects motivation. So that annual performance review you get, in the absence of any kind of goals, really does nothing to help you improve your performance.

This may seem counterintuitive until we realize that it's really goals plus feedback. It's having a target to shoot for, followed by feedback—some evidence that tells you how well you're doing. Are you in the bull's eye, or are you in the outer circles? How on target are you? Or to use an analogy from the sport of running, is your time approaching the time you've set as a goal for yourself? Whatever measurement tool you use, it's necessary to have both goals and feedback.

Measurement systems, therefore, are really essential whenever we're implementing our plans and trying to determine progress. The organization that's the very best at this is the SRC Holdings Corporation. Years ago, Jack Stack, who was one of the co-founders of that organization, established a process whereby everybody—every single person in this engine remanufacturing company—gets together once a week to evaluate how well their specific units are doing, compared to the goals they had set. They compare that week's performance to the previous week's as well as to how well they've done over the course of the entire year. They provide that information, which is then processed and fed back to them in an organized fashion. They call this process "the great huddle," and it happens on a weekly basis. That really is the way to do it. Anyone who wants to know how to implement a plan effectively really would learn a great deal from taking a look at what they do at SRC Holdings.

Wright

I've seen companies hit a home run with a project but never really understand how it happened or how they could learn from their success. What are your recommendations for organizations in terms of gaining the maximum return from their efforts?

Kouzes

We've found that the best leaders are also the best learners. Therefore, the best leaders always take the time to debrief both failures and successes. I think the most important thing we can do to maximize our efforts is to treat every activity, whether it's a success or failure, as a learning experience. We often say that experience is the best teacher. That's only partially true. Experience can be the best teacher if you take the time to learn from it. But if you just have an experience and then keep going, you're going to keep repeating the same mistakes. The key to continuous improvement is to be able to step back and take a look at the lessons you've learned from those home runs you've hit as well as from those strikeouts. It's hard to repeat a behavior if you have no clue as to what's contributed to its success. You've got to stop the action, pull the project team together and ask, "What did we do well? What did we not do so well? What should we do differently next time?"

Wright

In your experience, what is the single most important consideration for organizations seeking successful organizational change and better results from their efforts?

Kouzes

Trust, trust and trust. People won't change their behaviors unless they trust the people initiating the change. In our twenty years of research, we have learned again and again that the single most important portable leadership quality is one's personal credibility. People who don't believe in the messenger will not believe the message. So unless people trust the leaders, unless they trust the team members, and unless they trust the organizations not to punish them but to support them if they fail, people will not innovate.

Research on innovation clearly shows that there's a positive correlation between risk and trust. The more you trust, the more you risk. So only organizations that score highly on trust in both their management and their team members can be highly innovative as organizations. And I would add that you cannot do it alone. Change requires collaboration, and collaboration outperforms individualistic achievement or competition.

Wright

Jim, it has been an absolute delight speaking with you today. Thank you for your time, for your information and for your inspiration.

Kouzes

It's been my pleasure, David.

Jim Kouzes
1784 Patio Drive
San Jose, CA 95125
Phone: 877.866.9691, Ext. 239
Email: jim@kouzesposner.com
www.leadershipchallenge.com

Chapter 5

DON HUTSON

Don Hutson is an internationally known author, speaker and business trainer, who has addressed more than two thirds of the Fortune 500 and is featured in over 100 training films. He is chairman and CEO of the Memphis-based U.S. Learning, past president of the National Speakers Association and is in its Speakers Hall of Fame. *Don is the author of* The Sale *and* The Contented Achiever *and is a member of the prestigious Speakers Roundtable.*

David E. Wright (Wright)

Don Hutson, CPAE and CSP, is in the business of making people believe they can do better, and he gives them the skills to do it. For over thirty years, he has energized his audiences into action. He successfully worked his way through the University of Memphis, graduating with a degree in sales. After becoming the number one salesperson in a national training organization, he established his own training firm. Shortly thereafter, he was in demand as a professional speaker. Don's dynamic programs have garnered him several honors and awards over the course of his career. His peers elected him to the presidency of the National Speakers Association and he has received the prestigious Cavett Award as Member of the Year. He was also honored as the annual recipient of SMEI's International Speakers Hall of Fame award. Today, he is the chairman and CEO of U.S. Learning, and has made over 5,000 speaking appearances. Don is also regularly featured on national television and currently serves on five corporate boards. Don is the author of *The Sale* and co-author of five other books. Don Hutson, welcome to *Taking Charge*.

Don Hutson (Hutson)

Thank you David. I am delighted to be with you.

Wright

Don, throughout the business world, you're known as someone who delivers real solutions for business professionals. In your opinion, what are the most critically important attributes of an effective leader?

Hutson

I think first and foremost, a leader has to have committed followers. I think there are some people who might have a title implying a management position or leadership responsibility but at any given moment might look back only to see that no one is following. To be the kind of leader today that's got committed followers, I think we must have a leadership style that really works. A style that gains the commitment of our people will not only individually empower them but make them proud part to be a part of that organization. When people feel that they are a part of the vision, they will perform better.

Wright

I remember a man told me many years ago, "David, if you think you're a leader and you look around and nobody's following you, you're just out taking a walk." It's been said by many people who teach leadership skills that the leader must set the standard in a company. How does one develop his or her leadership style?

Hutson

I think first of all a leader must build a strong foundation on integrity and character. I used to say that in passing, but in today's business world, it is more critically important than it has ever been. We've got to understand that what's right is more important than who's right. What principles we subscribe to are more important than this quarter's earnings. If we can set standards for ourselves individually in that manner, we're going to build an organization that is, indeed, postured for growth and progress. So we can't have a flighty approach to building an organization today. It must be based on strong standards, and we must be the kind of person who people will enthusiastically follow. There are many attributes of a high-performance leader today, and I would say that would be the first. To cover a couple of others, I think we've got to understand that the same things don't turn all people on. We should manage people individually rather than manage and lead people en masse. When it comes to policies and procedures, we need to have some consistency and certainly a code of fairness, but when it comes to really getting inside someone's head and getting the most out of him and helping him grow, I think we need to do it with a focused individual perspective.

Wright

I would agree with you on the character and integrity issues. It seems that we're living in a time when some of our national leaders are making decisions based on public opinion. Do you think integrity and character are things you can develop late in life, or are you born with it? How would you suggest that those of us who want to become leaders develop these kinds of characteristics?

Hutson

I asked somebody one time, "What's the best way to gain wealth?" and he said, "Choose your parents very carefully." To take a chapter out of Dr. Bill Bennett's philosophy, the greatest way today is for us to make sure as leaders, as parents, as managers that we're setting the proper example. As trite as it sounds, I think a lot of that has to begin at home at an early age. This is not about adolescent leadership, so I won't elaborate on that, but I think that's a great starting point. Can we develop it later in life? Absolutely. We are indeed the sum total of the exposure we've gained and the decisions we've made. As we make decisions, we've got to do so with a high level of consciousness and a focus on a noble goal or vision. That means, yes, the development and the nurturing of unswerving integrity and essentially doing the right thing is more important than it's ever been.

Wright

Don, many times things go wrong in America's companies, and failures are often reported. In your opinion, what is the single most costly mistake that leaders and managers make?

Hutson

I think the biggest mistake they can make is to lose sight of the feeling, thinking and behaving of their workforce. It's been said that in Japan, people look out a hundred and fifty years in their thinking for long term planning. In America, we're obsessed with what's going to happen this quarter! What are our earnings per share going to be? When we get so intensely focused on earnings and things related to cost cutting, because we're so focused on the moment, it is easy for us to lose sight of how our people are feeling and thinking. In sales training, I tell sales people not to ever give a sales presentation without asking needs-analysis questions first. Similarly, in management, I think we need to give our people opportunities for authorship. Let's tap into the collective intellect of our team and ask them what is important now. Let's find out what they think our vision should be, how we should go to market and what they are hearing our customers say they want and need. To do that, we've got to get out there on the firing line. I think we must avoid being a stealth manager. That's a person who comes to work and goes into his office and closes the door and stays there for hours. The stealth manager is there; you just can't see him! The real managers getting results today are the men and women in leadership positions who are out there talking to their people, asking key and critical questions and letting the people know that the leader cares what they think.

Wright

This seems to parallel your philosophy of managing people individually. There's nothing more demoralizing than being in an organization where individuality is not respected.

Hutson

That can be a real demotivator, when somebody feels that he is being put in a pool with a lot of people less productive than he is, especially if he is getting the same earnings.

Wright

In your work with top corporations, you focus on the key indicators of the differences in people. Could you elaborate on what some of these are?

Hutson

One of the things I refer to quite often is that I believe strongly in management understanding the behavioral style of each employee reporting to him/her. I've been teaching the behavioral styles model called Social Style for many years. While Hippocrates was talking about similar concepts in 400 B.C., amazingly, it is very timely and beneficial material today. It's based on the behavioral style grid that has four quadrants: Driver, Expressive, Analytical and Amiable. Like a window with four equal sized panes, the grid is a square with four equal sized quadrants. The horizontal line through the center measures the degree to which people assert themselves, with the "Tellers" to the right extreme and the "Questioners" at the left extreme. The vertical center line measures one's display of emotion, with the "Reserved" types on the top and the "Emotional" types on the bottom.

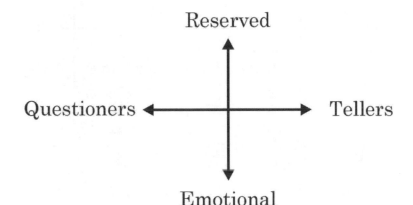

Given this framework, we have the means of evaluating each individual as to his or her resulting quadrant. In the upper right, we have the "Reserved Tellers," also known as Drivers. These people tend to be task-oriented and generally have a short attention span. They come on strong and are competitive, challenging people who have a low display of emotion.

Then in the lower right corner of that grid, we have the "Emotional Tellers," also known as Expressives, who are usually enthusiastic and focused on dreams and goals. They come on strong with a high display of emotion.

In the upper left on the grid, we have the "Reserved Questioners," also known as the Analyticals. They're laid back, have a longer attention span and are into facts and logic. This, along with their low display of emotion, makes them appear introverted to most.

In the lower left quadrant we have the "Emotional Questioners," also known as the Amiable. This person displays emotions very readily and is quite relationship-oriented. They have a low tolerance for conflict and a high need to get along with others.

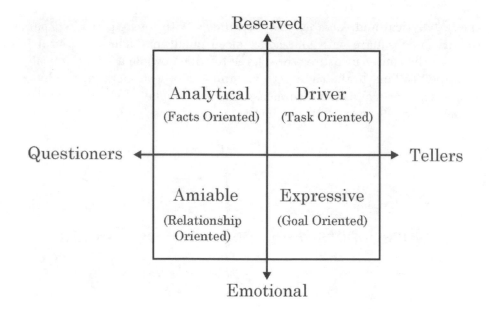

The neat thing about this grid is that every organization, of any size at all, has all four quadrants represented, except in extremely rare circumstances. That can give an organization excellent balance, because when people are psychologically and behaviorally coming from different places, they have somewhat of a different perspective on things. So that's the good news. The bad news is that the manager has really got to give a lot of thought as to how you manage, motivate and communicate with all of those different people differently.

Wright

So what you're saying, then, is that of these four distinctly different styles of behavior, one is no better than the other—just different.

Hutson

Great observation. There is no best place to be on that grid, because everybody has strengths and everybody has weaknesses. The really astute and observant manager is going to have a real good handle on what the individual employee's style, strengths and weaknesses are. You've probably heard the old cliché, David, that the most successful people are the individuals who build on their strengths as their foundation for success and very insightfully identify and manage their weaknesses. They eliminate them when they can but at least handle them well if they can't totally eliminate them. Managers must help their people do that. That's what the coaching component of leadership is all about. That's also the reason why, if we manage or lead people with distinct differences en masse, we're in trouble.

Wright

If I wanted to try to figure out which style I was so that I might be able to understand myself better and work on my strengths, how would I go about that?

Hutson

There are a couple of ways you might consider. One, you could have a discussion with your people in a staff meeting where you're talking about this concept and ask each other for feedback—questions like, "Where do think I am on the grid and why?" are good. This needs to be an open forum, with each participant being willing to embrace and learn from the feedback. Another way is to utilize available tools—I use these in seminars—where we have what's called a style identification checklist. It gives you a process whereby you will be able to actually run them through a Style ID Checklist chart by making some decisions about the observable behaviors of people. The result of that chart tells you which quadrant they're in. It's a soft science. It's inexact. It's imperfect. But nevertheless, it's a valuable tool. The most accurate way to identify one's style is throughout the utilization of a formal feedback process. At U.S. Learning, we have what we call the P.S.A., our Personality Style Assessment. It is a Web-based assessment product, and with it, you come into our Web site, and we then give you the opportunity to be profiled through this assessment process. That gives you the opportunity to do two really neat things. Number one, you spend about three or four minutes and fill out what's called the Self-Report. Answers to those questions quantify which quadrant you're in based on your own perspective. Then we have the Observer's Reports. You e-mail those to a number of people, and they fill it out based on their perception of your communications style. After they do that, you see on your computer screen all of these little dots on the grid that tell you where these other people think you are. So there's some interesting feedback that we're able to gain through that process.

Wright

Could you tell our readers how they could find that Web site?

Hutson

Yes—www.uslearning.com is our Web site, and you'll see Personality Style Assessment and can go right into it. There is a nominal charge, and for a period of several days, you can send that to an unlimited number of people. You can also vary it by constituency. You might want to e-mail twenty to customers, telling them you would like to get their input on their perception of your behavior. You could also e-mail ten or twenty to co-workers, family members and friends. Then you can profile it by constituency. This is a way today, David, that we can gain immediate feedback from others and learn how our communications style really works!

Wright

Don, how does one's style of communication and behavior differentiate him or her from others?

Hutson

The four styles I've just described are pretty easy to observe over a period of time, enabling us to understand which quadrant somebody is in. After you observe his or her style, the key is for us to then alter our style to be effective with that person. One analogy people often use is the concept of the chameleon, the small lizard that changes colors based on its environment or the background behind it so that you can't see it. Mother Nature has given the chameleon that unique protection device. I think in interpersonal communications and being an effective leader, we need to be almost chameleon-like in our communications approach. It's not manipulative and it's not trickery; it's just being an effective communicator concerned about the comfort of the other person. That's a very key concept we call adaptability, also referred to as flexibility. Regardless of the quadrant someone is in, he or she is going to have an adaptability rating. Whatever quadrant they're in is okay. In terms of adaptability, however, we want to make sure we're more adaptable rather than less adaptable. If we are seen as less adaptable, we're perceived as inflexible, rigid, unmoving and unwilling. That tends to turn people off today. On the other hand, if we're seen as more adaptable, we come across as flexible, pliable and willing to adapt and to do the things necessary to make the other person more comfortable. I'll never forget, I was in a board meeting one time and someone said, "Well, I think we need to do so and so." This one person in the meeting said, "Oh, I don't think so. We don't want to become victims of our own rigidity." I made a note of that phrase and thought of how indicative it is of some people whose lack of willingness to work with others causes them to be victims of their own rigidity! Today, in the interpersonal arena, we need to be flexible, adaptable and certainly not rigid. We all know that change is inevitable, but progress is not. We must consciously work at it.

Wright

Rather than being manipulative, it sounds like with this system, you're just trying to speak to people the way they want to be spoken to.

Hutson

That's exactly right.

Wright

I was told by a man many years ago that as long as I used the other person's language, he would understand me better.

Hutson

That makes sense. In fact, we have a segment of this subject matter we refer to as Strategy Keys for Adaptability, and I'll briefly share them with you. Generally speaking, you want to be efficient in communicating with Drivers, because they want to know the bottom line, they have a short attention span, and you want to minimize the amount of time you spend rapport building. With the Expressive, we need to be stimulating, because if you're not, they'll be thinking about something that is. So you need to keep their attention and present your ideas with enthusiasm and focus on the vision for the future. With the Analytical, conversely, you need to be accurate, and enthusiasm, frankly, can be counterproductive. You need to be calm, accurate, detailed and present the specifics of in-depth data. Then with the Amiable, we want to be agreeable and avoid confrontation. While the Driver wants to attack the task, the Amiable wants to make sure that all of the people involved are comfortable. So in this light, Drivers and Amiables are opposite and Expressives and Analyticals are opposite.

Wright

You really helped me and our readers understand the different styles. Can you tell us which one is best suited for business success?

Hutson

Good question. I stand by the premise that there's no best quadrant to be in. You have people with high work ethic in all quadrants and people of low work ethics in all quadrants. There are many other factors, so we don't really say that there is predictability about more success by quadrant. Until we get to that factor I mentioned called adaptability. That's quantitative and qualitative. We do want to be more adaptable. There is predictability that a more adaptive communicator or leader will be more successful than one who is less adaptable. So that's the big differentiator.

Wright

What are your strategies for developing and using the most effective leadership style?

Hutson

Let me give you some of the ideas that relate to managing and motivating different people differently. To manage an employee who is a Driver, the best advice is to give her direct instruction. Say, "Here's what we need to do..." and don't beat around the bush; just offer direct input.

With Expressives, the recommendation is to give them goal-focused guidelines. "If we commit to this plan and all do our part, we'll be able to reach our goal!" That's what they really identify with.

Conversely, the Analytical is more focused on historical data. That factual information has high credibility with him. So we accurately communicate with Analyticals, giving them written, detailed input, because they respond to data more so than the feelings.

Then to manage the Amiable, we want to focus on their commitment to teamwork. "You know, what we need to have you do, Susan, is so and so. If you'll do that, that's going to be the greatest contribution to this team effort." That's what gets the Amiable to respond. So those four skills represent how we can manage different people differently.

Now, to your other question, we also have varying skills for motivating different people differently. To talk about them briefly, you want to motivate the Driver by recognizing his impact on results. Remember, they are results- and bottom-line-oriented people.

With Expressives, you motivate them by giving them public recognition and opportunities to be recognized and praised.

With the Analytical, you want to relate to the principles they believe in. Again, we're back to hard data, information and beliefs.

And with the Amiable, we motivate them by emphasizing the positive outcomes with others, because that's what represents their highest priority.

Wright

It seems to me that if I had four people whom I was dealing with or managing, I would get great mileage out of having one from each quadrant.

Hutson

That's right. Can you see here where the biggest problem might be our tendency to manage or motivate everybody the same way, which for many, many years is what a lot of leaders and managers have done? Today, there's just more detail required to do it right.

Wright

If you were a supervisor at a large company and you were in charge of putting teams together, how much emphasis would you give to putting people with different personality styles together? Or would you try to group them together?

Hutson

I would tend to have some variability on each team, because they bring different value and perspectives to the table, which might well result in better problem solving strategies. If everybody on the team is an Amiable, for example, you're only going to have one perspective, which might be rather limiting.

Wright

What guidelines can you offer our readers? How do we go about doing all of this?

Hutson

I would simply suggest that in the recruiting, selection and interviewing processes, you try to gather enough information to get a good handle on what someone's style is. While you wouldn't want to decide to hire someone or not based solely on her style, you would want to make sure that her contribution to a specific team effort is going to be maximized.

Wright

Our company is in a growth mode right now, and we're hiring a lot of people. We've made two fairly major mistakes in the past year.

Hutson

Hey, that's called "paying your dues" in leadership. Way to go, David! I'm really glad that you've not been deprived of that learning experience!

Wright

We fixed the problems pretty well, I think, but I read recently that in the interviewing process, the interviewer is talking ninety percent of the time and the person that he's hiring is talking ten percent of the time.

Hutson

Which is exactly how you're not supposed to do it.

Wright

I should have read that a year ago.

Hutson

It's been said that the important thing about interviewing is that you're trying to speed up your learning process about that individual. That's the reason why the questions you ask need to be penetrating ones, the answers to which give you insights into their abilities.

Wright

That's great. What other principles can you share with us?

Hutson

I think we really need to respect the dignity and individuality of everybody we manage. That means that, whatever his style is, if we're not careful, we can go into a reactive mode and say, "You know, Charlie is weird." Well, what does weird mean? Weird means they are different from us. But let's not look at that as a negative when it can certainly be positive. The old Southern comedian Brother Dave Gardner used to say, "Everybody's weird once you get to know them!"

Wright

He was one of my favorites, by the way.

Hutson

He was great. He thought he was being funny, and everybody laughed at it, but I thought it was deep psychology. When you really get to know people, you identify their idiosyncrasies. The more things we can learn about people, the better we're going to be able to communicate with them. So we need to respect their dignity and their individuality, regardless of where they're coming from. I think a couple of the other things we need to do as managers and leaders is be able to create great and positive energy in our organization. We are indeed creating energy at all times. The question is, is it positive energy or negative energy? The great leaders and managers of the business world today are able to create positive energy. They get people to respond positively and to get energized and excited about something. They get their people to buy in and become the real committed champions of an organization. If we don't have the skill as a leader to achieve that, we're going to end up with a bunch of apathetic and unproductive employees, who respond negatively to input and are low energy. That, of course, is counterproductive to success.

Wright

What a great conversation. I really appreciate you taking the time. It's always a pleasure. I've followed your career now for years and years, and you really seem to have your thumb on the heartbeat of management training.

Hutson

I appreciate your saying that, David, and I would close with a quote from Elbert Hubbard, who said, "It's a fine thing to have ability, but the ability to discover or develop ability in others is the true test of leadership."

Wright

That is well said. Don Hutson is in the business of making people believe that they can do better and gives them the skills to do it. We really appreciate you being a part of *Taking Charge*.

Hutson

It's been my pleasure.

Don Hutson
U. S. Learning, Inc., Sales Growth Specialists
516 Tennessee St., Suite 219
Memphis, TN 38103
Office: 901.767.0000
Email: Don@DonHutson.com
www.USLearning.com

Chapter 6

TERRI MURPHY

Terri Murphy is one of the industry's leading consult-
ants and published authors on the integration of tradi-
tional marketing and communication with today's
Web and Internet tools. Her expertise is developing
and growing customer relations to create a more
profitable business model for Fortune 500 corpora-
tions and sales companies. She is the CIO for U.S.
Learning, Inc. and a frequent spokesperson
for sales industries nationwide.

David E. Wright (Wright)

Today, we're talking with Terri Murphy, a communications expert and sales entrepreneur who built a highly successful business over the last twenty-four years. Today, Terri helps individuals and businesses learn how to work smarter and not harder by consulting with them on the most effective ways to use e-mail and the Internet to build the virtual side of business that increases profits and expands traditional marketing. Terri Murphy is a national communications consultant, best-selling author for Dearborn Financial Publishing and an accomplished columnist, television producer and national presenter. She is an active member of several national and state sales and commerce organizations. Terri Murphy, welcome to *Taking Charge*.

Terri Murphy (Murphy)

Thank you.

Wright

Terri, taking charge or leadership in business today is probably neither harder nor easier than in the past. I do, however, think it's different. Would you agree that the Internet has changed the way most companies do business?

Murphy

The Internet has changed the way we do business forever. Immediate results, instantaneous communication and real-time service are the new norm. The newly-empowered consumer demands new criteria for service and is not willing to settle for less than immediate, easy results. I would say it's required us to do business in a different way. No one could possibly ignore the challenge of conducting business in a global network as opposed to a local one, which has forced businesses to think outside the box. The Internet offers us the miracle of communicating instantaneously, for the price of a local phone call, with anyone, anywhere in the world, at any time. Today, we must implement and effectively use systems that can handle the increased volume of connectivity and improve customer relationships while keeping the communication personal. As with any new revolutionary communication tool, we must realize that everyone is not at the same level of Internet proficiency. Many businesses often miss the simple step of maximizing the use of e-mail to make their Web presence profitable.

Wright

I know I am, but I was dragged, kicking and screaming into the Internet business, actually.

Murphy

Most of us were dragged into the confusing world of technology, with many challenges of understanding what to buy, who to buy from and how to use it. Nobody wanted to spend that much money on something they couldn't measure or understand. The Internet does truly offer an easier, simpler and more economical way to connect and sustain relationships. When the Internet first launched for general public use, I was in a top sales position and quickly learned that I needed to communicate with people the way they wanted to be communicated with, regardless of the tool. Communicating with people the way they want to be communicated with is not only a gracious thing to do but serves the very core of meeting and exceeding the new consumer demands and offering the contact in a style and a method that serves their individual needs. The Internet gives us an opportunity to communicate with people and offer ongoing value-added information to create a relationship for life. The ease of the Internet provides a way to nurture relationships in business that was never available before.

Wright

Early in your career, you learned to build strong customer networks to ensure success. Is using the Internet a better way to connect with people today?

Murphy

I learned the value of building a strong customer network because I was terrified of not being able to make a living. I learned to use connectivity in an ongoing way that added value considerably past the original service. The Internet today is not necessarily a *better* way, but it is *another way* to connect with people. When I consult with medium size or small companies, the goal is to help them provide valuable, targeted information to their client, customer and prospect base, to position them as a truly valuable *resource*. This new position offers us a way to connect with lots of people at one time, in an individual way that was previously too difficult and expensive to accomplish. By continuing a relationship beyond the original service, we, in fact, build a longer lasting relationship and maximize a higher level of client and customer loyalty, thus saving us money. Direct mail was a type of "broadcasting" and resulted in a small return on the investment of time and money. To send out fifty letters would take a greater investment of time and money. Sending out to fifty targeted e-mail contacts is relatively simple and cost effective. When done correctly, electronic communication has really improved results and increased the probability of retaining clients and customers. Unfortunately, many businesses today are hiring expensive tech consultants who do not possess marketing savvy, thus missing the brilliance of creating online marketing. We should all be promoting the uniqueness of our brand using effective e-mail and Web solutions that serve the emerging empowered consumer, enabling us to build a database by using some of the e-tools available today.

Wright

And to be so inexpensive—I mean, the communication tool, as it relates to money, it just fascinates me. I was surprised the first time I got an order over the Internet for our books—the questions I had. How in the world did they find me?

Murphy

Businesses are learning that just having a site on the Web isn't proving profitable. However, they are not asking the right questions when they secure a Web site. The key to an effective Web presence is to incorporate a unique selling proposition to make it easier for clients and customers to find and use your services on the Web. A large part of being an entrepreneur is offering a distinction in your business model and maximizing how you provide service to meet and exceed today's newly empowered consumer.

By studying these new demands, it is apparent that although you may conduct business locally, you are now competing in a global arena and must gear up to meet customer demands in a twenty-four-seven format. Offering full services and instant information online meets the demand for real-time commerce, regardless of regular business hours or time zones. Businesses must now provide a twenty-four-hour service model that effectively works globally while you are not. The advent of the Internet can provide a twenty-four-hour service level if you set it up correctly and without a huge investment. It is imperative that the Web site does more than offer information. A Web presence without the ability to capture and continually serve a customer is a waste of time and money.

Many people do not understand how to develop a unique online brand that supports how they are found on the Net. They ignore the true way to drive traffic. A primary key to driving Web traffic is to directly target the resources of your own sphere of influence. This is supported by giving a consistently refreshed value-added support to encourage returning to the site for additional information and services. Most businesses continue to underestimate and undersupport the value of past clients and customers and focus on getting new ones. By incorporating a few key guidelines to your marketing tools, both on and offline, you will drive and build traffic to your site. The next step, of course, will be to keep them returning again and again, even if they are not necessarily interested in your basic product or service. Associating affiliate and peripheral resources that save time and offer benefits with you or your company's services easily creates return traffic.

Wright

Can you give our readers a few tips on how to build a full and strong Internet presence and use Web tools to build their business?

Murphy

Our recent e-book offers a couple of easy-to-follow guidelines to help build and sustain a full and strong Internet presence. Remember, you need to serve your clients and customers around the clock by incorporating as many of the new consumer demands as possible in every facet of your service. These demands encompass: speed, convenience, options, ongoing added value, discounts, quality information and extreme service. I'll break down what I mean.

- **Speed:** Everybody wants what they want fast.

- **Convenience**: They want whatever they want when they want it, which makes it tough for a regular salesperson working only during designated business hours.

- **Options**: Clearly, the Internet has given us the ability to profile different sources and products against each other so we can be more discerning about what we want.

- **Add Ongoing Value**: For the first time in business, we are easily able to offer multiple opportunities to provide resources and information through automatic response software that provides reports on demand. This value-added capability will allow us to share our alliances through cross-marketing services. We are now collectively able to create new opportunities, new powers, new accomplishments, because I can connect you with resources of my own. Value-added service is evident in many franchises today that have learned to serve multiple needs with a singular location. Taco Bell and Baskin Robbins® tandem up to co-market two different food services, and it has proved to be a highly successful venture. Borders® bookstore has challenged the giant online book provider Amazon® by offering a combination of products and lifestyle. Cross marketing not only serves the core business but minimizes costs and provides a better consumer experience. This is part of the collective power of people lateralizing and cross marketing each other's opportunities for business.

- **Discounts (and Premiums)** are another opportunity to leverage the customer database of one company while expanding the value of another company's services with a premium or discount for the end user. The Internet serves us with a paperless way to reward consumers with discounts and preferred pricing when we tandem our data mining with others that have the ability to serve another aspect of the consumers' needs. It is not necessarily about cutting out the middle man, but it's clear that securing a product directly is faster and often less expensive. We are willing to pay more for convenience. You'll pay more for a cup of coffee at a Four Seasons than you will at a gas station but it's what *you* are willing to pay. Offering preferred pricing or premiums is an important opportunity, because I can literally use my influence, my database, my sphere and my position to get you more business. Discounts also apply in how we can help people stay connected to maintain relationships. Technology offers us ways to offer online coupons for services like free long distance for an hour to a client or customer who's still in the process of making a decision or a free cup of coffee while they think it over at a Starbucks via a printable coupon. Businesses will be able to offer ongoing discounts and services continually *after* an initial sale. We are finally understanding the value of a client or a customer beyond the initial transaction. That client or customer has invested time and energy in you. There's a trust there, and it should be valued and respected. I think that's where true leadership comes in.

- **Quality Information** and what I call **Extreme Service** round out the platform, which is what business is all about, delivered in real time *connectivity*. Design your service model to deliver as many of these demands as possible simultaneously, and you have created a differentiation to your services. Here are some of the ways you can do this.

  o Build a permanent online brand by creating a domain that brands the service/person.

  o Use business providers that can host that domain and "point" to your Web site.

  o Publish and use only permanent e-mail addresses within your company that brand you and your service easily and memorably.

  o Use Client Relationship Management tools and software to sustain/nurture/leverage past clients/customers/prospects.

  o Incorporate value-added reports and information via Auto Responders with Client Capture software to maximize and effortlessly build on customer visits. Develop these reports with specific attention in the construction of the reports to secure traffic via search engine and directory searches.

Wright

I've bought the last four or five computers that I own on the Internet, and I was writing these down—speed, convenience, choices, value added, discounts—and almost every one of those applied. That's why I bought those computers.

Murphy

Exactly! You were seduced by the ease of purchasing, with enough information to make an informed decision, and so the platform offered you real *service*. Today, people are numb to the words "great service." because after the initial sale, the relationship is often abandoned and nothing happens to wow them. When you find a real integrity to the offers of true service, there's an authenticity, a realness to what people are trying to do, and that attracts consumers, because they know it's in their best interest. Web tools, used effectively, can provide the individual, real-time needs of the masses and work while you sleep for a modest investment.

Tracking this activity and studying how people want to be served helps guide us with future marketing strategies designed to make the process easier and more inviting. It is after the sale is made that the true client relationship management begins. We are now able to really track the value of a past customer and know that the relationship can result in thousands of additional dollars in sales through cross marketing and valuable referrals.

We are finally able to understand where our business is coming from with the electronic tools that are available through a well designed Web site and use of e-mail.

Wright

It's been said that the person least likely to know how to operate a computer is the owner or the boss of the company. How can you help those of us who are techno-timid to do more than just be online?

Murphy

It is imperative to understand that in the world of e-communication, all e-mail messages are essentially publishing. For that reason, any company needs to establish a simple guideline to ensure that the communications sent from their locations are professional and appropriate. When used effectively, all e-mails become a prospecting tool, and with a few special tweaks, a company can increase the effectiveness of its marketing and cut costs dramatically when using e-tools to promote the company and its products and services. The key to professional e-mail messaging is that the e-mail address be permanent and brand the company, which requires a couple of initial steps.

- The company should register its name as a domain name.
- The company should have the domain and Web site hosted to create online recognition of the company e-mails, with the main domain default being .com whenever possible.
- The company should synergize its e-mail and Web addresses with the company name in the domain name: marys@shoestore.com and www.shoestore.com, for example.

The costs are minimal, and the results *huge* when a few important key steps are implemented early in the game. Regarding a full Web solution, the best advice I can give an owner of a company is to do a little homework and ask the tech designer the right questions to help create a profitable Web investment. I find from my consulting business that more often than not, an owner hires a Web designer and doesn't know what he expects the Web solution to do for the business. Too often, he or she invests a lot of money in a fancy "virtual brochure" on the Net. The tech designers are masters at building Web sites but may not have the touch of including a friendly, simple format for easy navigation and simple functionality of the site. Before hiring a Web designer, it is imperative to ask the right questions to get the right outcome. Here are a few considerations to make the transition to using the Internet and Web tools easier and more effective.

- Develop a detailed company electronic policy that will address the new lead generation and sales through the Net. Identify issues like procuring cause, response time, Spam and e-blast policies, personal employee e-mail guidelines, follow up and after-the-sale CRM to protect the company and other employees.
- Select a Web solution that does more than perform like a Yellow Pages ad that incorporates Web communication tools like auto responders and automated reports to meet and serve clients' and customers' real time requests for products and services.
- Create and brand an HTML e-mail newsletter template directed at clients, customers and prospects that offers value-added service and

new information and is in a format that establishes immediate recognition that brands the company's logo colors and styles.

- Require the Web site to have full client capture of visitors that helps build an online database or listserv®.
- Request that the site be designed to have a full "back end" work station for non-tech access to make simple information changes.
- Insist on the use of e-mail addresses that brand the company via permanent e-mail addresses and pointer domains that clearly identify the company and the employees and enforce the company brand.
- Implement the use of mail managers to handle electronic online filing of all e-mail messages. Require all employees to use full information signatures on all incoming and outgoing electronic communication that include "hot links" to the company Web site and the sender's e-mail address to peruse their present business model and see where the company can think outside the box to provide a quicker and better level of service and resources to customers and past customers on a twenty-four-seven basis.
- Implement an aggressive CRM (Client Relationship Management) plan to reclaim and maintain past clients and customers in order to construct a strong database that can leverage future zero-based marketing, communication and services to that database.

Wright

That leads into my next question. I was going to ask you about name recognition. Name recognition seems to be one of the most important tasks a leader has to establish to be successful these days. Is it possible to develop an online brand and unique selling position?

Murphy

Branding goes beyond a catchy phrase or smug by-line. True branding is an underlying philosophy of how a business is known and presents itself, as a brand is nothing more than helping people identify what you do and how you do it. A great example is the company that manufactures the Rolls Royce automobile. The double "R" symbol represents a full host of implications like luxury, quality, status and commitment to excellence. Another great example of branding is creating a distinction in how your services are delivered. Domino's Pizza created a most distinctive niche in the pizza delivery arena when they branded delivery in a specific time frame. That special segment of the product and its delivery creates a "USP" or a "unique selling proposition" to the consumer. This distinction helps brand the company and its product in a new and consumer-serving manner. With statistics revealing that we are bombarded with over 400,000 bits of information daily, it is imperative that companies study the needs and habits of their consumers. A company must fill the need and do it in a way that is distinctive.

Wright

Has the Internet—with its ability to reach the masses—made it easier for women to succeed in business?

Murphy

As a woman in business for more than twenty-three years, it is my observation that what the Internet offers is a level playing field. The small biz entrepreneur, whether a woman or a man, can compete on the same "digital field" as a Fortune 500 company, provided they use some of the important guidelines we are discussing today. I have helped many companies and organizations create a higher profile and strong niche by helping them to analyze and fulfill the expectations of the clients and customers they want to serve. Recent surveys show that there is a strong surge in women-owned starter companies. The Internet is a great way to market and offer products in an economical way. In addition, women very often have multiple roles in life, like mothers, wives, et cetera. The Internet provides flexibility of access to any global network from anywhere in the world, including personal home offices.

Wright

The reason that I asked the question is that women who seek leadership positions seem to have an uphill climb, considering the fact that if they work outside the home, they are still expected to be a mother or a wife in the traditional sense. How do you help women accomplish a life balance?

Murphy

When used effectively, the electronic tools of today minimize costs and maximize time and effectiveness, which, when well planned, afford any business person the opportunity to continue to be highly involved in their businesses without having to actually be on premises. A comprehensive business plan should include substantial virtual office services that allow for products, services and communications to be secured online. This diminishes the need for huge staffs and large warehouses of inventory. Client and customer communications are fast and simple and can target hundreds of contacts though electronic messaging in almost no time and very little cost investment. This streamlining of e-commerce offers us the opportunity to structure our work around our real life and can be done from anywhere.

Since the Internet never closes, it becomes imperative that we design our work and real life with guidelines and boundaries that serve us first. This window of choice allows us the opportunity to give ourselves permission and time to take care of our families and ourselves. When boundaries are firmly in place, it is simpler and easier to create the critical balance that is so necessary for our quality of life to flourish. Authentic personal power flows from a sense of calm, health and self-respect. One of the best examples is from Dr. Stephen Covey's Book *The Seven Habits of Highly Effective People.* Dr. Covey suggests that we plan our calendar "backwards," placing the most important items on our calendars first before plugging in the work. It is exciting to be enthusiastic about serving clients and customers, but it is just as important for us to take care of ourselves so we can provide more creativity and better services and perform at our highest and best.

Women, in general, just need to take even fifteen minutes of quiet time to focus on the fact that they *are* the power. I don't mean powerful in a negative way but rather that they have the power within themselves to take care of self first. It is a choice to be full within and then give gifts to others. In too many cases, women are pushed to unattainable limits of being superwoman and miss the many gifts of the journey and miss living a rich life. One of my favorite authors is Sarah Ban Breathnach, and her super successful book *Simple Abundance* is excellent. It is one of the most focusing "real-life" books on self care that I can recommend.

Wright

One attribute that successful leaders and managers seem to have in common is the ability to communicate effectively. You seem to advocate communicating with different people differently. Can you explain what you mean?

Murphy

Early in my career in sales, the first four people whom I worked with were actuaries. If you spent any time with me, you can tell I'm just fully expressive, enthusiastic and outgoing, which is pretty much the opposite behavior from their introverted behavioral style. I was challenged by people who didn't relate the way that I did. A true leader realizes that there is graciousness to communicating in the way people want and need to be communicated with. Different people process information differently. The Internet gives us the opportunity, for instance, to serve many ways of engaging communication, which includes voice, text and HTML or graphical communication. We have the ability to communicate with people in a way that makes them feel comfortable, which establishes a level of trust and empowers them to help us help them. If people are not comfortable with you, then there's no sale, and there is no quality exchange, and the relationship is often doomed. It is imperative that we understand and accept our own communication style so we can better communicate and serve others.

Many of my clients request our program on effective communication by understanding the different ways different people need to receive information. This is highly apparent today when we are using e-mail in a "flat text" format. Again, considering the new consumer demands, when communicating with people in a way they find compatible with their style, you bridge the gap of words and phrases by offering information and services in a way that creates a richer and more mutually beneficial approach. The basis is not new, but now more than ever, it is imperative for us to recognize and respect the differences and individuality of the people we serve and that we deliver our products and services in a way that is comfortable and gracious to that person. Our program for Communicating with Different People Differently is one of our most successful and requested programs.

Wright

Do you use anything specifically as instruments, like the DISC or the Myers-Briggs, or do you have your own system?

Murphy

Technology, again, has helped us fulfill a traditional need with a new delivery method. Terri Murphy Communications offers a comprehensive twenty-nine-page online personal assessment that offers action plans and is quite detailed about helping the participant understand the strengths of his or her communication style. The assessment also allows the participant to glean responses from observers as well. By understanding how others perceive our style, we then move forward with a better self understanding to enable us to be better observers and more intuitively sensitive to how we impact others.

Wright

In an article that you wrote for the popular business magazine *PC World*, you stated that consumers, thanks to the Internet, are now smarter than many of the small businesses trying to serve them. How do you suggest small businesses reverse this trend?

Murphy

A good percentage of our consumers are very comfortable using the Internet as a medium, which is a shift in how information is accessed. Many businesses are still in denial about what they need to do, because they still have business as usual, not realizing that this shift grows incrementally every day. It's like not building the ark, because it's not raining. The small business entrepreneur definitely needs to understand that he or she has to create an Internet presence, which includes a full Web solution. It may or may not need to be full online commerce, but it does need to provide contact information about the company and services outside of regular business hours and offer value-added reports and interface.

E-mail connectivity with permanent e-mail addresses served by business Internet Service Providers need to replace content providers and ISP account temporary e-mail addresses.

Getting into the e-commerce world in a most basic premise requires five keys to be in the game. Just like you need a phone and a fax, you need a permanent e-mail address, Web services and resources. When consulting with the small business entrepreneurs, we help expand on what they already have or guide them to services and systems to help build their customer database and serve customers and clients using tools that work for them when they are closed. It's essential for survival, as the population fully integrates the Internet to be in the loop. We now know that the ability to track that client can be worth $45,000 over the life of the relationship and that it's costing $200 to make the phone ring. To compete and flourish, the small business entrepreneur, which is what the country was built on, must take advantage of this window and begin integrating his traditional services and marketing a solid e-presence. The first step is to begin, and that is as simple as picking up the phone, calling past clients and customers and asking for their e-mail addresses when updating their records. Ask permission to send them information electronically and begin building a viable, clean database. This is the foundation to beginning a strong e-commerce level to any business, and, as always, it begins with personal communication.

Wright

What do you think are the attributes that make great leaders? What do you think is the major difference between a manager and a true leader?

Murphy

A true manager shows leadership qualities when he or she understands that it is not about them. True leadership creates a space that empowers others to build something together that is bigger than a singular effort could do. Most people are doing the best they can with the resources they have. If you have a company or a group of people that are not working well together, there is a reason. It's always based on understanding and wanting to be understood. When people feel they are understood, they are more likely to open up. A good leader, in my opinion, is sensitive to the needs of other people and goes out of his or her own way to understand how to empower people to achieve a higher purpose. A truly successful manager inspires people to aspire to high achievement and become their own personal best. Most people are eager and open to non-manipulative guidance. I think a good leader will help people see how they are a significant piece of a puzzle, how their unique contribution is critical to that puzzle and how their contribution is totally unique. A true leader will help create the vision that each individual has an impact and creates an eternal conduit of impact that helps whomever they connect with to have better lives. It's not about intimidation; it's more about recognizing that leadership creates a brand new reality for these people. It helps lead them to a destiny that maybe they never gave themselves permission to have. It's not about, necessarily, self-importance; it's about an experience of going beyond interdependence into being the best person that we can be in part of a larger theme. A good leader recognizes that there's a gift in every person, good or bad, strong or weak, and that there's a lesson to be learned. I like the quote, "There's a pony in the pile; we just have to find it." It takes those tough experiences to affect a new learning experience. I think we learn too late in life that we storm trooped through a couple of really good learning experiences and to view those experiences not as victimization, but as brilliant opportunities. Leadership goes beyond positive thinking in that every challenge presents a new way of learning or looking at something differently. You mentioned that you interviewed Deepak Chopra. Deepak has a most riveting quote about failure in his book *Creating Affluence*. He says, "'F' stands for the fact that in every failure there is a seed of success. In the manifestation of the material from the non-material of the visible from the invisible, a fundamental mechanic is involved. This is the principle of feedback. Our failures are stepping stones in the mechanics of creation, bringing us ever closer to our goals. In reality, there is no such thing as failure. What we call failure is just a mechanism through which we can learn to do things right." There's just feedback from the non-material to the material that it's not the way to do it.

I think a good leader helps you focus on the end result and to improve the process as it integrates with your personal growth to achieve the results that serve everyone involved with a win-win outcome.

Wright
What an interesting conversation. I really do appreciate you taking time to talk to me today.

Murphy
As we say in Italian, *"Molto piacerre!"* (The pleasure is mine!)

Wright
We have been talking to Terri Murphy. She is a consultant, a professional and a best-selling author. She is an accomplished columnist, television producer, national speaker and, as we have found out today, a very intelligent entrepreneur. Thank you so much, Terri, for being with us on *Taking Charge*.

Murphy
Graci, David.

Terri Murphy Communications, Inc.
An affiliate of U.S. Learning, Inc.
516 Tennessee Ave., Suite 219
Memphis, TN 38103
Office: 901.767.0000
Fax 901.767.5959
Email: terri@terrimurphy.com
www.terrimurphy.com

Chapter 7

GEORGE RITCHESKE

George Ritcheske is a consultant, executive coach and speaker with more than twenty-five years' experience in developing leaders and building high-performance leadership teams in financial services, insurance, real estate, manufacturing and service industries. He is adept at aligning workplace efforts with strategic plans to meet current objectives while implementing change for continued success. He captivates his audiences with stories drawn from his experiences in business, as a Scoutmaster and as a dad of twins.

David E. Wright (Wright)

Today, we're talking to George Ritcheske, president of TrueLeaderCoach, Inc., which provides executive coaching, leadership team effectiveness and people-development programs and services. He earned a BA in economics from Dartmouth College and an MBA with an emphasis in organizational behavior at the University of Michigan. He is an active member of the National Speakers Association, the International Coach Federation and the Organization Development Network. George Ritcheske, welcome to *Taking Charge.*

George Ritcheske (Ritcheske)

Thank you, David. It's great to have the opportunity to share insights about leadership.

Wright

George, in researching your book *True Leaders: How Successful CEOs and Presidents Make a Difference by Building People and Profits*, you started with a group of leaders who, by reputation, valued people as well as profits. Was this attitude a common thread through all of the leaders you interviewed?

Ritcheske

Yes, David. The inspiration for doing this book came after the dot-com bubble had burst and we saw that there were so many leaders who seemed to be motivated by greed. We were looking for those leaders who were building their businesses for sustainable success and who were genuinely caring about people. So we asked our colleagues for recommendations on people who were successful in the corner office, cared about people and believed their people made the difference in their business. We were looking for those leaders who were building people. When you build people effectively and fully engage their talents in providing quality products or services to customers, profitability is what follows as your reward.

Wright

So these people, in effect, were recommended before you even talked to them.

Ritcheske

That's correct. We also had each of them complete a values assessment before we interviewed them so that we had a clear understanding of their underlying motives. The results reconfirmed that their interest in people was both genuine and significant.

Wright

Without mentioning any names, I was interested in whether or not you found some people who had been recommended but who were not what they seemed to be, and so you left them out of your book.

Ritcheske

We did have several who were recommended, and after they saw our profile, that we were looking for leaders who really cared about people as a key part of their approach to leadership, they politely declined. Also, if an assessment didn't match up with the profile, then that leader was left out of our book.

Wright

I was interested, when I read the book, that with one person, it was just impossible to get through all the gatekeepers that surrounded her, so you left her out.

Ritcheske

We discovered that true leaders were very accessible and were not surrounded by gatekeepers keeping information from them. In fact, that openness to information is a key characteristic of the leaders we interviewed.

Wright

As you interviewed the twenty-seven leaders for your book, did you discover any core values that they shared in common?

Ritcheske

We sure did, David. In the values assessment instrument we used, there are six values. Four of these values surfaced as the dominant motivators for true leaders. The top value for our true leaders is "Social," defined as "an inherent love of people and a genuine desire to lift and develop the potential in others." This value is very much other-focused. The second shared value is what is called "Utilitarian," defined as "a value for money and a return on investment, whether time or money; a measure for practicality and results." So our true leaders were very pragmatic in that sense. If they're investing time or money, they expect a return, because that's what the shareholders or the folks who provided the capital expect in any business—a return on their investment. Third, interestingly, is the "Individualistic" value, which is "a desire to have the power to control one's own destiny and influence the destiny of others." If this one is too high in the values ranking, then you get a "me-first," or "me-only," kind of attitude. We think this is what led to a lot of the CEOs who are currently in disgrace because they were focused only on their own wealth, or the wealth of a few. However, with our true leaders, the position of the "Individualistic" value shows that they want to influence the direction and destiny of others and themselves, because they believe they will able to do it for the greater good better than others. Finally, the fourth value is "Traditional." The folks who developed the assessment believed that "Traditional" was representative of leaders who were generally resistant to change. In fact, what we found out through our research was that these were not leaders who were resistant to change but rather who saw the value of following timeless principles, even during changing times.

They had a belief system that said there are right things and wrong things. As a true leader, you emphasize that the right and the wrong is unacceptable. So there is a really strong sense of ethics, integrity and doing what's right.

Wright

I had a minister tell me many years ago, "David, some things are right, no matter if no one does it, and some things are wrong, no matter if everyone does it."

Ritcheske

That's a great way of saying it. When we asked our true leaders what was unacceptable within their organizations, they would respond with such answers as lying, cheating and stealing. That just was not acceptable.

Wright

I suppose of all those values, I would be not bothered by, but maybe stalled a little bit, about the "Individualistic."

Ritcheske

Businesses operate in a very competitive environment. The "Individualistic" value is really a necessary component, because in any organization, as folks are moving up the ladder, they're competing with other candidates for those leadership opportunities. We found that our true leaders needed this value to be able to compete for those leadership roles but that it was moderated by their belief in other people and the traditional value of doing things right. So it was a positive influence within the organization.

Wright

I was interested in a remark made by the president and CEO of Hallmark Cards.

Ritcheske

Yes—that is Irv Hockaday.

Wright

He believes that leaders need to create an environment that allows talent and leadership potential to develop, excitement to occur, teams to form, dialogue to go on and mentoring to happen. Did you find that the leaders you interviewed gave their employees the same opportunities?

Ritcheske

We found that the true leaders really enjoyed creating environments that allowed people to flourish. Jack Kahl, who founded a company called Manco, told us how they handled moving into a new office facility. Jack said, "You know, every business has some office map. We decided to create a community, and in a community you have street names. We had the folks in the business create the street names and the names of the departments. So they had fun creating the names, and then each group decorated their area according to the name they had picked. It was a fun way, and yet it also had an underlying principle of building that sense of team, where we each have our areas but are also building community where we invite others to come see our part of the neighborhood." Kip Tindell and Garrett Boone are the co-founders of The Container Store, which has been rated one or two in Fortune's 100 Best Companies to Work For in America for the past four years. When we talked with them about their environment, they said, "Well, let's give you a specific example. We had a woman who was working in the accounting department, and she came to us and said, 'I really think I'd like to work in the warehouse.'" Now to them, it was not something they ever would have thought about. They talked with her, and she said that she really enjoyed working with her hands and had this organizational capability. They said, "Okay," and they moved her into that area and provided her some additional training. She is now the manager of their warehouse system.

So as they said, "We can't tell what people are going to be best at. We have some ideas, but it's really up to them to be working on things that they really enjoy. Through that, they can contribute to the success of the organization." We found true leaders looking for opportunities to help people grow beyond what they were doing into roles that utilized their strengths effectively. We also found a very strong emphasis not just on mentoring but also on coaching. Mentoring says, "Let me share with you from my experience so that you can benefit from it." All of the true leaders, I believe, want to do that regularly. It is why they participated in our project—to share wisdom and insights with others. The coaching process then equips the leader to help other people grow faster. The coach helps individuals see what they are doing in a different way and emphasizes how the individuals can build on their strengths and how they can manage around those gaps that they are still developing.

Wright

Did you find any instances where this characteristic of mentoring went beyond the corporation? Did it go out into the community as well?

Ritcheske

We know that our true leaders are involved in the community. They have a sense that through their leadership positions, they have opportunities to access information from people that others do not and a real sense of obligation to share with others what they're learning. We also found that the true leaders were humble. We would ask them about themselves, and they wanted to share stories about other people. We found a real strong sense of humility. We talked to John Bruck, chairman and president of BHE Environmental, Inc., a company in Cincinnati that provides a full range of professional environmental and remediation services. John told us he surrounds himself with people who are smarter than he is. He said, "When I do that, it gives them the opportunity to really make a great contribution in their area of specialty." Then he said, "It's up to all of us to really make a difference in the work that we do. In environmental services, there is a very strong emphasis on doing things that really improve our environment."

Wright

The first principle in your book is passion. Could you tell our readers how leaders are guided by their passion, and is it really necessary for success?

Ritcheske

It depends on how you define success. We define success as "really making a difference on a sustained basis." We believe that passion is absolutely a prerequisite. When we talked to Len Roberts, the chairman and CEO of Radio Shack Corporation, we asked him "What's the purpose of your business?" Instead of the typical answer, "Oh, it's to make money," his response was, "Our purpose is to help demystify technology for the mass market." Then he said, to put it more simply, "We want our customers to be able to come into a Radio Shack store and get their technology needs met without being made to feel stupid." When we asked him "Who are the heroes in your business?" he replied, "Oh, absolutely the store managers. They're the ones who hire the team, develop the team and create the environment that our customers experience when they come into the store. It's that experience that either keeps customers coming back or scares them off. So our store managers really are the ones who make a difference in our business every day, and everything in our organization then has to be designed to help our store managers do their job best."

Wright

I was interested in the word "sustained" when you talked about success. A lot of people have success, they peak, and then they rave about it for the rest of their lives. You're talking about something that, over time, would show that someone affected the business world or the environment in some way.

Ritcheske

That's right. During our interview with Jim Copeland, the CEO of Deloitte & Touche, we asked him what his advice would be to leaders who believe they have become successful. He looked back at us, smiled and said, "Don't breathe your own exhaust, because as soon as you start believing that you are the smartest, the best, that's when you've stepped over the line into arrogance. You stop learning. You stop listening. You stop leading."

Wright

I've often heard that the difference between leadership and management is vision. Do you find this to be true?

Ritcheske

What we found is that it is not just having a vision; rather, it is having the ability to find and to see the trends and then lead processes within the organization to help people understand the implication of those trends on the business. It is that capability that we found repeated over and over again as our true leaders would talk about how they regularly ask people questions such as, "What's happening here? What implications will that have towards our business?" Because it is through those kinds of questions that they help people get out of, "Well, our business is successful today," and into, "How are we going to change and evolve and grow to meet the needs of customers tomorrow?"

Wright

So to be excited about one's own interests, it is necessary to always be getting more information or knowledge.

Ritcheske

Yes. David Novak, CEO of Yum Brands, Inc. —formerly Tricon Global Restaurants—said it very clearly: "As soon as you convey in your organization that you're the smartest person, you're the person who fixes the problems, that is the day that you put a cap on your organization's potential. Because now people will come to you for the answers, and they'll expect you to have the solutions. The business world is changing too rapidly. There's more information around than we can possibly analyze, and you have just capped the potential of your organization."

Wright

You have written that true leaders must be powerful communicators. What, in your opinion, is the most powerful communication tool a leader can use?

Ritcheske

The most powerful tool is listening.

Wright

Listening?

Ritcheske

Listening. And it's listening generously. As Frank Hennessey, one of our true leaders, said, "When we generously listen, we are learning. We are gaining from the other person's perspective and the whys behind their perspective. So when we listen to customers, when we listen to suppliers, when we listen to employees, we really do gain a better understanding of how people see our business, how they value our business and how they want to be involved in our business. So it is through that listening that we are learning what to do next." Lou Smith, who runs The Ewing Marion Kauffman Foundation in Kansas City, said, "A leader listens, learns from what he or she is hearing and then has earned the opportunity and right to lead."

Wright

Learning seems to be important to leaders. Could you give us some examples of how the people you interviewed felt about training and knowledge?

Ritcheske

The principle that we expressed in the book is called "Treat Learning Like Dirty Dishes." It actually comes from Linda Huett, president and CEO of Weight Watchers International. She used the food analogy to say, "You know, after a great meal, we want to relax and pat ourselves on the back and say, 'Oh that was great' and when it's a bad meal, we just want to forget about it or put the blame on somebody else." She said that in business we do the same thing. "We have a great success and we pat ourselves on the back. If we have something go wrong, then we want to place blame or just forget about it. What needs to happen is that leaders and their people take the time to reflect on each experience. What went wrong? What can we learn from that? What went right, and how can we continue that? What can we change to be more effective? We have to do that after every good thing or bad thing so that we're extracting the maximum amount of learning out of that situation to apply to our next effort. It is that next effort that either continues to improve our business or causes us not to be as effective as we could be."

Wright

Would this be the same thing as brainstorming in reverse or reflecting throughout the company?

Ritcheske

Yes, and reflecting is something that we do not do very often. We are so driven by tasks that we finish one and move right on to the next one. Yet it is that reflection time that allows us as individuals and as groups to really extract the maximum learning out of each task, project or experience. What went well, and how can we replicate it? What could we do differently to be more effective? Put those new ways of operating into effect, because what we're delivering today, either a product or service, met yesterday's customer's needs. That's when we identified it, and it takes time to develop and get it to the market. What we have to be doing, then, as we are conducting our business today, is developing what our customers are going to expect tomorrow.

Wright

I have been booking speakers for about thirteen years, and I have found that in bad economic times, the first thing to go is the training budget.

Ritcheske

We found the opposite of that at The Container Store. When we asked them what they do in a business downturn, Kip Tindell looked at us and said, "We train our people more," and when we asked why, he went on, "Because business is a cycle, and in a downturn, what you want to do is prepare your people for when the upturn starts. When the upturn happens, it's like a wave. You can either surf the wave, because you and your people are ready for that new wave, or it will be a wave that will smash you. We'd rather surf on the next wave."

Wright

I remember when, as a young man in the late '60s and early '70s, this company came to me and wanted to sell me some training materials, and I made the mistake of telling them I didn't have the money for it. The representative looked at me and said, "I know; that's why I'm here." So I found a way to purchase it, and it did change the complexion of my company. So these leaders, then, believe so strongly in training and knowledge that even in the downtimes they step it up. Would that be one of the differences between true leaders and just positional leaders or managers?

Ritcheske

Yes, because they recognize that knowledge is indeed power. What you want to be able to do is create powerful people throughout your organization. We found that true leaders are really focused on helping people develop their competence so that what they are offering is high quality, their confidence. So they will offer their talents and their character so that they are doing things in the right way.

Wright

You know, we've seen leadership by poll taking in our political leaders in the recent past. According to your book, true leaders tell the truth. Did that surprise you?

Ritcheske

It was something that we were hoping to find, and we were reassured when we did. Mike McCarthy, who is the CEO of McCarthy Building Companies, told a story. He said he had over expanded his business early on in his career; there was a business downturn, and he had to lay people off. Rather than delegating that to somebody else, he went out and told each person who was being affected that he or she was being let go because of his mistake. He said, "I made the mistake. I over expanded. Because of that, I have to let you go. My commitment is that I am going to rebuild my business, and I would be honored if you would consider coming back to work for me when I do that." Well, he did rebuild the business, and many of those folks did come back. McCarthy Building Companies is now is one of the top ten U.S. general builders, and they have a wonderful family atmosphere. It is built on trust, because Mike McCarthy tells the truth. Jim Copeland of Deloitte & Touche said, "You know, we can tell people all sorts of things about what's happening within our business, but if we don't tell them the truth, then we are not respecting them. People deserve to know that they're being let go because of something they did, in which case they have accountability for it and have to change it in their next opportunity. And if it is due to business conditions, we should acknowledge that, because they shouldn't have their esteem knocked away because of mistakes that we've made."

Wright

How do true leaders demonstrate and build trust in the work place?

Ritcheske

We found that there are many trust-building tactics, such as sharing responsibilities so that you are giving a vote of confidence to someone and open communication about what is happening with the business. This open sharing of business information was emphasized time and time again. Jack Lowe of TD Industries, which is in the top ten of Fortune's Best Companies to Work For in America, disclosed that they share everything in their organization except individual compensation. "You know, our competitors might get that information, but the truth of the matter is our people need that information in order to align what they do daily in ways that will help our business." Jim Nicholson, president and CEO of PVS Chemicals in Detroit, has "Call Jim Day" once a quarter. These are days when he's in the office and employees—or their spouses or even their kids—can stop in or call in to "vent or praise or complain." He also spends a full day with new employees in the organization as they join so that they understand the priorities in the business and have a personal relationship with the CEO. He also emphasized the sharing of business operating information as he said, "When we share information and share the rewards, people will align what they're doing in ways that will be beneficial to the organization, to our customers and to the employees themselves."

We also found another trust-building tactic, and it is not really a tactic but a true strategy of recognizing people who are doing good work, since by doing that, you help build them so that they can contribute in other ways as well. David Novak, the CEO of YUM! Brands, Inc., tells a story of when he was working for Pepsi. He had moved from a corporate role into an operational role and was trying to learn everything that he could about merchandising. He was sitting around a table with a group of merchandisers, and they were all sharing their stories about how they had learned from Bob and how Bob had been so helpful in coaching them or mentoring them or sharing his expertise. David looked up and saw Bob at the other end of the table, and he had tears rolling down his cheeks. David looked up and said, "Bob, what's wrong?" Bob looked back and said, "David, I've worked in this organization for thirty years, and I never knew anybody cared." David told us that's when he made a transformational decision, "If there is nothing else I can do as a leader, I will recognize people who are doing good things for the organization. That builds trust, because now you're really focusing on people who are doing the right things in the right ways for the right reasons, to not just please customers but to delight customers, to provide something that really is better than the competition."

Wright

George, you state that true leaders trust their intuition and are willing to take risks to meet the challenge of change. I've never heard intuition discussed in a business setting. Can you explain what you mean?

Ritcheske

Intuition is that inner voice that speaks to us. The dictionary definition of intuition is "an ability to know something without the conscious use of reasoning." We have also heard it referred to as gut instinct, judgment, wisdom or an inner knowing. Intuition is not shooting from the hip or guessing but rather combines experience and learning to enable a leader to trust that inner voice that says no when all the facts may say yes. Kip Tindell, a co-founder of The Container Store, shared their six "Foundation Principles," one of which is, "Intuition does not come to the unprepared mind." What leaders need to do is read more broadly. They need to talk with people with different perspectives, and expand their experiences, because it's through that that leaders can develop and then listen to that inner voice. In today's business world, it is easy to get overwhelmed with all of the information that can be analyzed and cut and pasted any number of different ways. Developing one's intuition will help sort through that overload quickly to figure out what really makes sense going forward. Kip gives the analogy of fly fishing. "I think I'm pretty good at it, and if I intuitively think a trout is under a rock and I cast over to it, there is probably a trout under the rock. The likelihood is that it's there, because I have read, I have experience, I've talked to others, and that's now part of my informed intuition. But if you have never fly fished before and you intuitively think there is a trout under the rock, there probably isn't; you would just be making a wild guess." So he said our intuition is developed, and then we have to listen to it. Jim Nicholson of PVS Chemicals said he has been growing his business through acquisitions and discovered early on that the surprises after an acquisition are always negative, never positive. So if the numbers tell him that it is a good acquisition to make and his gut is telling him that it's not quite a right fit, he'll go with his gut and say no, because it is after the acquisition when the negative stuff comes out. By the same token, he said, "If the numbers are telling me that it's maybe not a good deal and yet my intuition is telling me there's something there, then that tells me the organization probably has some very good people who haven't been well directed. I can make an acquisition there, because I know that I'm adding resources to our business." So intuition is that inner voice that helps us cut through the information overload and be able to make incisive decisions more quickly. We believe that in our fast-paced business world, it is a characteristic that needs to be developed more fully, because we're overanalyzing ourselves. It's paralyzing us in terms of being able to make good, quick decisions.

Our true leaders also emphasized how important it is to take risks to respond and grow. We all tend to get into our comfort zones. We have to stretch ourselves, step out of our comfort zones and into our "learning zones." When leaders and their companies stretch, they are learning things that will help them respond more effectively to the changes in the marketplace

Wright

Your tenth and final principle is to "Respect the Importance of Balance." How does this apply to true leadership?

Ritcheske

We found three aspects of balance to be important to true leaders. As my son pointed out to me when he was fifteen, we are following Aristotle's Golden Mean—everything in balance. The first aspect applies to personal balance. Are we living to work or working to live? Gary Nelon, chairman and CEO of First Texas Bancorp, Inc., said, "I think that if your organization is made up of unbalanced people who aren't taking good care of themselves physically, who aren't taking care of themselves spiritually and who aren't renewing their minds constantly, trying to increase their education, then something about the overall organization is not going to be in balance."

The second aspect relates to the organizational balance between the needs of customers, employees and shareholders. As Tim Webster, president and CEO of the American Italian Pasta Co., describes it, "The true challenge of a leader is to find and maintain the optimum point for balancing the needs of these three groups. If you give into any one group, you will take away from the others, and you business will less successful."

The third aspect is what we call "world balance"; that is, balancing the needs of the company, of the community and of the environment. When we asked David Walker, who is the comptroller general of the General Accounting Office (GAO) in Washington, D.C., about his leadership mentors, he responded by first telling us about the president he most admired, Teddy Roosevelt. "President Roosevelt believed in a strong national defense, because he said we lived in a dangerous world, and he believed in protecting the environment, because there is only one world in which we all live. He didn't think we should do one or the other. He knew we needed to do both." In the same way, true leaders are always seeking win-win solutions.

Wright

What an interesting conversation, and what an interesting book. I appreciate you sending it to me. I found it very interesting.

Ritcheske

That is great to hear, David. We believe all of us need positive role models, and these twenty-seven leaders have shared wonderful stories, wisdom, and insights.

At the end of each chapter, we included an Explore and Discover section containing a series of coaching questions to help readers find applications to their own situations. We found successful people in the corner office who care about people and would share their stories and insights about why the ten True Leader principles are important, how they personally demonstrate them and how they operationalize them within their company. Any leader or aspiring leader will find inspiration in these stories. Then through our Explore and Discover section, readers are able to find applications in their own situation so they can continue to build on their capabilities on their journey along the true leadership path.

Wright

I plan to use those, right after I go buy a couple of highlighters.

Ritcheske

That would be good, David.

Wright

The next time you see your book, there will be a lot of yellow in it.

Ritcheske

We have discovered that folks are finding that it is a great gift for others, and many readers have found that as they go back and read parts of it again, with their additional experience, they're coming back and saying, "Now I understand what that means," or "Now I see a way that that could really be applied in my own situation, in our own organization." We have also gotten a universal response that we need true leaders in our businesses, in government, in our schools and in our churches.

Wright

Today we have been talking to George Ritcheske, president of TrueLeaderCoach, Inc. He is also the author of *True Leaders: How Successful CEOs and Presidents Make a Difference by Building People and Profits*. George, I really appreciate you taking this time today for this conversation. Thank you so much.

Ritcheske

Thank you, David, for the opportunity to share the *True Leader* message. I absolutely believe we need true leaders in all of our organizations, in all walks of life. True leaders care about people, and they care about uplifting everybody around them. We sure need more of that in our world.

George Ritcheske
Williams Square Center
5215 North O'Connor Blvd, Ste. 200
Irving, TX 75039
Phone: 972.304.6137
Email: george@trueleadercoach.com
www.trueleadercoach.com
www.true-leaders.com

Chapter 8

BILL STIEBER, PH.D., CSP

Bill Stieber, Ph.D. is a consultant and trainer who has more than twenty years experience showing America's top corporations leadership, teaming and improvement methods that have increased perform-ance in financial services, insurance, healthcare, manufacturing and service industries. Bill is an ex-pert at orchestrating workplace dynamics. He has an innate understanding of how the rhythm and mel-ody of each workplace create harmony and ulti-mately greater success in organizations.

David E. Wright (Wright)

Bill Stieber, Ph.D. and a certified speaking professional, is an interna-tionally recognized business consultant, trainer and author. A former Dem-ing Consultant, Bill's expertise over the past twenty years enables him to bring enormous wisdom and insight to his clients. His musical talent makes him uniquely attuned to incorporate rhythm and harmony, or lack thereof. By imparting practical strategies through musical metaphors in his high energy entertaining presentations, he delivers substantial content and en-gages his audiences. Bill ensures immediate applications in the material by promoting audience participation. His fresh approach enables him to facili-tate more effective work places. Dr. Stieber's professional background in-cludes many quality, training and organizational design and development assignments. In these roles, Bill has developed team and leadership compe-tencies, totally redesigned major business units, implemented performance management, peer and leadership feedbacks systems, including 360-degree assessments, conducted leadership assessments and developed a new management and team training curriculum for a merged Fortune 500 organization. Bill Stieber, welcome to our program this morning.

William G. Stieber (Stieber)

Good morning.

Wright

Did you begin as a musician, or were you just playing in college. How did that happen?

Stieber

Actually, my music was first. I started as early as twelve years old, when I played the clarinet. I played classical music with school bands and orchestras. I continued playing clarinet for a number of years. At sixteen, I started playing tenor saxophone. Also during high school, I became involved in the choir. We sang competitively in the Philadelphia area during my early high school days, and I continued singing. Actually, as I was going through college, I played in wedding bands to help pay for college expenses. I continue to be involved in my church. I play in the folk group monthly. I play bass guitar. I play a number of different instruments and continue to sing from time to time as well.

Wright

I'm always looking for recruits. I direct three choirs myself, and I'm always using instruments out of the Knoxville Symphony Orchestra. I always like to test the competence level.

Dr. Stieber, several years ago, Alvin Toffler, the futurist, wrote about change. He was more concerned, though, about the rate of change. Are American corporations suffering from ever-increasing technology advancements, or is it simply that human nature resists any kind of change?

Stieber

I don't believe that American corporations are suffering from technology advancements. I believe their suffering comes from their inability to plan and implement other features necessary with change, what I call the organization system elements that are needed to transition that technology change effectively in their companies. In the face of the human nature, there is always resistance to change. Leaders must identify what outcomes they are seeking as a result of implementing technological advances. I call this an outcome-based leadership approach. Some outcomes may be associated with business, such as increased profitability or decreased expenses. Some outcomes may relate to customers and deal with increasing customer satisfaction or decreasing dissatisfaction. And some outcomes may even be associated with employee satisfaction.

Now once these outcomes are identified, leaders need to be identifying the key behaviors, skills and other requirements needed to drive the outcomes associated with technological advances. They also need to identify the gaps from their current state to the future state of where they want to go. Then they need to get a better handle on the change required. Most importantly, they need to plan and implement changes, their specific initiatives and other organization elements to accompany the company technology change if they are going to succeed against this natural human resistance to change. Often, installing advanced technology involves answering questions in a number of areas, including decision making. Who will be responsible for all the key phases in implementing technology? In the people area, they need to ask some of the following questions: What skills will we need to successfully implement technology? How will we contract around performance using this technology? How will we train and implement ongoing coaching to ensure new technology skills remain current? From their organizational structure, they need to ask questions like these: How can we organize ourselves effectively to get the work done using their advanced technology? Perhaps most importantly, they need to think about reward systems. How are we going to formally and informally reward people for effectively using the behaviors required to implement advanced technology effectively?

American corporations suffer from this change, because they are often poor implementers. They forget about Murphy's Law. Instead of asking what can go wrong with implementing new technology and developing appropriate preventative and contingent actions to each ensure the success of their plans, they implement plans and continue to fight fires based on the resistance of humans and other factors not effectively planned for during their implementation of technology.

Wright

You mentioned the word "leaders" and also "management" and "end results." I was told the other day by a management consultant that the difference between management and leadership was that leaders had vision. Is that what you are talking about when you say "end results"? Would that not imply that you would have to have vision?

Stieber

Yes. I think that is a big difference, and leaders have to have that vision of what outcomes they want. They ask, "What are the behaviors that will drive us to this change, to these outcomes? What are the organization's components required to drive those behaviors?" They also need a vision that motivates and inspires people.

Wright

In a book you co-authored called *Thriving on Change*, you quoted from a recent survey on human resource professionals that reported only thirty-seven percent rate their companies positively on communication efforts regarding the change process. In fact, twenty percent said "poor" or "very poor." Do you think this is accurate?

Stieber

I will be honest with you. I certainly don't think things have improved in our statistics. In fact, I think that if the survey were done in 2003, the percentage that was rated poor might have even increased a little bit. In almost every organization I worked with, either large or small, communication efforts regarding change remains a high problem area. I typically hear this problem of poor communication pronounced in a variety of ways throughout organizations that I work with. Poor communication still exists and surfaces in many different organizational situations. Just the other week, I heard people were caught by surprise about some organizational announcements. Obviously, some prior communication should have been transmitted earlier. In one mid-sized company, a top leader changed the title of the people in another manager's entire research department, causing stress among his managers. The department manager didn't know anything about it, causing a significant anxiety among the professionals that report to these managers, because they were unaware of it as well. Yet this was being announced to the whole organization without consulting the research people impacted.

That is just one example. I also see that many projects in organizations are developed and implemented around change with very little developed in the way of communication plans. Who does what, when and how frequently is eliminated or really not dived into a lot. They talk about the steps of the project but never about the mode of communication or the way things should be communicated around a project or change. Also, groups that are identified as key stakeholders are sometimes impacted by change but never informed. As a result, the change process bogs down or is delayed, because the stakeholder was not identified earlier and that stakeholder now raises some bad flags or resistance about the change. I also believe that many organizations do little to monitor the effectiveness of their communication efforts and the change process. So feedback is ignored or corrective actions aren't in place to deal with communication breakdowns.

Wright

Reading the same book, I got the feeling that you really believe in teams over individual efforts. Aren't teams harder to deal with from the management standpoint?

Stieber

Not necessarily. If you have the right structure, the right culture and the right norms in the organization, teams can be easier to deal with from the manager's standpoint. In fact, in some companies, I have observed teams that are almost self-management entities. The manager merely serves as a facilitator and coach to the group. The teams set their own goals. They plan and manage their daily work and in some cases even evaluate and give themselves performance reviews. The manager often helps teams secure the necessary resources and clears the obstacles that get in the way of the team's performance. Of course, in these team-based cultures, there's usually a strong believer at the top of the organization who sees the benefits of teams and supports that environment. There is also strong support for consensus decision making and typically a well-trained work force that can effectively communicate and give and receive back feedback effectively with each other. By the way, I am still a strong believer in individual effort. I do believe, however, we should reward and recognize both team and individual efforts when appropriate.

Wright

I was really interested in your opinion on that, because I have found that in selling, it's easier to sell to a group, for me at least, than it is to an individual. A group seems to relax more. They seem to be more open, and they almost sell each other. So I can see what you are talking about.

Stieber

Okay.

Wright

It was interesting to read your comments on total quality management and teams. You stated that sixty-four percent of companies that integrate TQM and teams report success, whereas only thirty percent of companies that did not integrate TQM with teams report success. How do you explain that?

Stieber

I think success in companies is often measured in dollars and cents as well as in improvements. While team implementations often show great results in these areas, those efforts that were focused more on key process improvement initiatives show greater bottom-line impact with increased customer satisfaction, increase in revenue, decrease in cycle time, decrease in expenses, improved processes and improved employee morale. The focus associated with TQM provides, I believe, a team integration of skills and expertise toward process improvements that often have a direct bottom-line impact and hence, greater success.

Wright

In your book, you name several types of teams including virtual teams, which, by the way, I had never heard of. Could you help our readers understand more about the differences?

Stieber

Typically in organizations, we have intact work teams that operate and get the work out the door on a daily basis. They interact and work together daily. But we also have a lot of ad hoc teams in today's work place. Project teams have a specific assignment to create a new product or do research in a way. We also have many quality improvement teams, and I think the modern day counterpart of that are Six Sigma teams, which you have probably read and heard a lot about today, that are responsible for improving a major business process and have a direct financial impact on the organization. Now many of these ad hoc project teams that I see are often virtual teams. In fact, I ran into one recently in a pharmaceutical organization I worked with. I often see a lot of them in pharmaceutical organizations but also in many other organizations. That is because of the fact that we have technology today. Virtual teams typically are teams that get together via technology. Much of their communication may be via e-mail or telephone. Many of their meetings may be conducted via teleconferencing, and many of the other team members are scattered in different facilities around the U.S. In the pharmaceutical business, I know there are a lot of virtual teams that operate on a global basis. So we may have a chemist in Paris, a researcher in the U.S. and a human resource person from the Far East that may make up a small component of this virtual team. I guess the only problem with virtual teams is that they don't get a chance to meet each other except via TV or computer. But I have seen their work, and obviously, a lot of organizations are using them when they have expertise scattered either around the United States or around the world and they want to pool that expertise. With the technology today, virtual teams may be an answer.

Wright

That's interesting. You state that trust levels fall during times of change. Since lack of trust is a significant issue, how do you counsel companies to overcome the lack of trust in their employees?

Stieber

Typically, I believe you need to train leaders on key communication skills to help build trust in organizations. I will work with leaders and help them engage in practices that promote a more healthy work climate. Some of that training also deals with minimizing trust-blocking situations, such as making sure that as a leader you stick with your commitments you make to employees, making sure you are not shooting the messenger, making sure that you are being straight and not sugarcoating responses to employees. Obviously, creating an awareness and conducting skill practices with all employees concerning active listening, feedback, interaction practices and communication styles, as well as other communication models, can also certainly help minimize this lack of trust. Obviously, based on some of the unusual practices we witnessed in 2002 in corporate America, maintaining an awareness of business ethics, I believe, can also help overcome that lack of trust.

Wright

I was fascinated to read what one team achieved in the steel manufacturing company. You pointed to it in your book. You reported that they standardized processes to reduce paperwork by sixty-six percent, and product development went from twenty-eight weeks down to nine weeks. How in the world is that possible?

Stieber

They lacked standardized processes. When companies lack standardized processes, it can cause great variation in your work flows and ultimately lead to significant costs. The reduction in paperwork largely came from reducing the number of tasks, which I refer to as non-value-added tasks, which were not needed to get the job done in the manufacturing processes. By decreasing a set of bureaucratic practices that was built up over a period of time—for instance, somebody might have suggested a certain form be used with a client fifty years ago, because it was critical to one event that suddenly became a new procedure that's done all the time—we are able to significantly standardize some processes down into what we call value-added types of tasks. In the company you referenced, automation also contributed to the paperwork reduction. A product development process reduction was achieved by taking a cross functional approach and focusing on reducing steps in the process flow, identifying clear roles or responsibilities around that product development process and developing procedures so everyone was consistently following the same process time and time again when they were developing products.

Wright

You have helped me, because my plan was to raise my chair behind my desk so people could see me over the mess. So now I will just standardize the process. Sounds like a better solution to me. No wonder you get the big bucks for consulting leadership. Dr. Stieber, I'd like to quote something from your book *Teaming for Improvement, Building Business Profits* that made a lot of sense to me. "When you see a group of beavers repairing a dam that has been hurt by rain, you see there is no real leader. The beavers work together as a team." Why can't people work as instinctively, or do you think they can?

Stieber

In this country, and I think in many others as well, the independent entrepreneurial spirit is alive and well. If we are raised in this type of culture, working as a team isn't instinctive and therefore requires us to behave a little differently. For some people, changing their behavior to adjust to a team-based culture is therefore difficult to do, and I know many decide to actually leave situations rather than adjusting that behavior to a level that would be uncomfortable. I have actually worked in an organization where they were moving to a team-based culture, and many people just opted out of the situation and took some kind of package from their company and decided not to work in that environment because of this entrepreneurial, independent type of preference that they had. Some people, because of their background or experiences, however, may actually operate well, and typically, they are the kind of people who think more collaboratively versus competitively. In these cases, team behavior may be more instinctive to them and, for this reason, less difficult.

Wright

As the head of my company, when I walk through and see something that needs to be done or to be repaired or fixed, I do it, repair it or fix it. I have often wondered why people don't just do things like that. But I have had some of these people walk through business life and say, "That's not my job." It is easier for me to think that people really want to get to the end result, but I guess if the leadership is not able to connect them mentally to the end result, then they will never be able to work instinctively. Is that true?

Stieber

Yes.

Wright

If you were building a team, would you use personality profiles such as the Myers Briggs Type Inventory or the DISC? Would that be important to you?

Stieber

Yes. It would. I am a definite believer in assessments. In fact, I've just developed, along with another colleague, close to twenty assessment instruments over the last couple of years. One of our most recent ones was called Self Assessment Inventory, 21st Century Leadership Practices. I am definitely a firm believer in people understanding their individual styles and preferred types on a team. It helps enhance effective communication with the team and with others outside the team as well. Team members and key leaders typically communicate with others based on their own developed and innate style. Once they are exposed to what I call the MBTI, or Myers Briggs Type Indicator or the basic DISC instrument, they develop an appreciation for the differences and preferences of others in their environment. By getting a handle on their own style, preference or type, they also can gain appreciation for their own strengths as well as opportunities for improvement.

They also gain appreciation for the potential conflicts associated with their own preferences when dealing with others. While the DISC instrument is helpful, the MBTI has a significant amount of research behind it and goes into great depth in understanding individual type. It is my preferred instrument to use when I am given the luxury of time to facilitate teams or team leaders. The MBTI results describe valuable differences between normal, healthy people. The differences can be a source of much misunderstanding and miscommunication among team members and between team leaders and team members. You can use the information to better understand yourself, your motivation, your strengths and potential areas for growth. It also helps you get a better understanding and appreciate others who differ from you. Understanding MBTI is self-affirming, and enhances cooperation productivity. It is used in a wide number of different venues, including self-development, career development, organization development, team building, problem solving, management and leadership training as well as a number of counseling areas.

Wright

It sounds a lot like diversity training as well.

Stieber

Yes. It can be used in diversity training, and it reports preferences on four scales, each consisting of different poles and providing insight into what you prefer. It really helps get a handle not only on yourself but in dealing with other people more effectively.

Wright

In your book, you dedicate an entire chapter to creative thinking.

Stieber

Yes.

Wright

By the way, I really did enjoy that chapter. Could you tell our readers how you would handle a brainstorming session for best results?

Stieber

I have had a chance to use it quite a bit over a number of years in the consulting and training areas. Brainstorming is a common method for a leader of a team or a team that creatively generates a high volume of ideas of any type by creating a process that is free of criticism and judgment. I enjoy this technique, because it gets all the team members involved and enthusiastic, and it encourages open thinking when a team is trying to break out of its same old way or paradigm of thinking. While there are two major methods for brainstorming, structured and unstructured, I prefer the structured, in which each team member gives his or her ideas in a structured way, as opposed to the unstructured, where team members give ideas as they come to their minds. That is easier to manage. I typically like to provide some time for key members to think about the brainstorming question or issue and then write it down for everyone to see. I may even want some of the team members to paraphrase the issue or question before recording it on an easel chart to ensure that everyone understands the questions. This time of reflection on the issue also recognizes those individuals on the team who have a preference for reflecting on issues. After some time, and sometimes it can be overnight or just a few minutes, depending on the time constraints, each team member in turn gives an idea, and with each rotation around the team, I give each member permission to pass at any time. I try to encourage participation so everyone is contributing. I write every idea on the easel chart or writing surface as ideas are generated, and it's important not to restate someone's idea but write it down exactly as you hear it. Don't interpret it. Avoid what I call "the power of the pen." In other words, you have the marker or pen, so don't abuse that power by writing things down differently.

I often check with the speaker to ensure that the idea has been worded accurately. I ensure that ideas are generated in turn until each person passes. I try to keep the process moving. In some cases, a brainstorming session may only last five to twenty minutes. I ensure that the list of ideas is clear, and I entertain clarification questions only during the process. Once completed, I'll work with groups to discard ideas that are virtually identical. If the list is substantial, I may even use a technique such as what I call "multi-voting" to reduce the list to a more manageable size, and I may even use such tools as an affinity diagram to group like ideas together, depending on the nature of the brainstorming topic.

Wright

That's interesting. If you were hiring people for a company, would you give more importance to attitude or to skills?

Stieber

I hate to give a consultant answer to this, but it depends. Actually, I think both are critical. Certainly, both are important in the work place. With organizations operating in a leaner fashion today, basic skills are critical. If I don't have the luxury, time or money on my side, if I were a company leader, I would probably look at the in-depth skills the person brings to the table. However, in the interviewing process, I'm more interested in a person's behavior and how he uses those skills to get results. In fact, I typically use a behavioral-based interviewing process to isolate specific successful or unsuccessful situations to discover how an individual dealt with a situation and assess his behavior and actual results obtained in a specific situation. These critical instances, I believe, are better indicators than mere skills and knowledge. I do believe, however, that attitude is even more important today than ever. There is a lot of negativity in the work place today. Negativity can block creativity and foster an unwelcome working environment. I therefore prefer people who have a positive attitude. It is certainly critical to positions that deal directly with customers.

Too many organizations leave bad impressions with customers, because they don't have the positive people to interact with their customers. Often these customers will tell their friends about this negative or less-than-positive interaction. Also, positive attitudes are more likely to enhance a healthy work environment, therefore making for a better place to spend your time. This can not only lead to higher productivity but also decrease costs associated with high turnover typically found in negative corporate company cultures.

Wright

I'm glad you answered the question honestly. When I have posed this question to other people, they have said things like, "Attitude is everything." But in one negative experience, recently, within the last year in our company, we hired this lady for a secretarial job, and someone forgot to give her a typing test. I don't know how in the world it got by us, but we hired her, and everybody loved her, but she just couldn't do the job. It was heartbreaking for me to have to terminate her. I hated it, you know, because I knew it was my fault. I spent ninety percent of my time apologizing and ten percent trying to find her another job.

Stieber

The interviewing process is very critical, and sometimes companies just don't spend the time investing in it like they should. Which causes some problems, like the one you faced, down the road.

Wright

With this book, of which this interview will be a part, we are trying to encourage people in our audience and readers to be better, to live better and be more fulfilled by listening to the examples of our guests. Is there anything that you could add that might help our audience and readers be better?

Stieber

There are certain key competencies that I promote in my sessions with leaders and teams that help others have better and more fulfilled lives. One of them is goal setting. In today's changing and turbulent world, we need to have focus. Too many people I interact with have problems setting priorities. I believe that by setting personal and professional goals, people can put a stake in the ground that will help them deal with direction and give them better directional focus. I also feel that by setting personal goals, they can launch a set of activities, such as more exercise or time with the family, that will provide a better balance in their lives and enable them to better cope with the stress that is rampant in corporate America today. I also believe that people need to think about their passion and give less credence to which job pays the most. I run into more well-paid people who are miserable about their jobs. These individuals need to get some help in finding out their own preferences and finding a good occupation that will fit with those preferences.

I also think that people need to better organize themselves by implementing tools and time-management techniques that will help them stay in control rather than being controlled. Typically, I find that if people can manage themselves, they are usually able to manage others and interact with others more effectively. I think people need to adopt a lifelong learning philosophy today. With change, we must continually improve and change as well. As individuals, we can often become stagnant. So I think people need to set themselves some learning goals and engage in activities, whether they be reading books, reviewing tapes or attending seminars that will keep them on the cutting edge and make them feel more fulfilled.

I think leaders need to think more systematically. When you want to make a change, think about the organization as a whole and what actions, whether it be communication, reward systems or decision-making processes, that need to accompany that change to make it an intrinsic part of the company. Too many Band-Aid solutions exist today that only cause more problems and pain in the work flow. Finally, I think people need to be more positive. If you have to, listen to positive affirmation tapes in the morning on the way to work. Catch people doing things right, and look for opportunities to reward and celebrate. It can be, I believe, a great antidote to the negativity that spreads in companies.

Wright

Bill, I certainly appreciate your taking this time to answer our questions and to be interviewed. It's been a real learning experience for me, and I really appreciate it.

We have been talking today to Dr. Bill Stieber, who is an internationally recognized business consultant, trainer and author and is the head of the company Orchestrated Dynamics, Inc. If you would like to know more about Bill and what he does, I would simply go to www.stieber.com, and there you will get all kinds of information and even free time-management tips. Bill, thank you so much for being with us today.

Stieber

Thank you. Have a great day.

Bill Stieber, Ph.D., CSP
PMB #3880
2865 South Eagle Road
Newtown, PA 18940
Business: 215.860.6098
Fax: 215.860.4398
Email: Bill.S@Stieber.com
www.Stieber.com

Chapter 9

CHARLES F. DAVIS

Charlie Davis is a consultant and executive coach who has come from the CEO Executive Teams. He spends much of his time training other consultants to do much deeper work with executives. Charlie specializes in the area of corporate strategy that most often breaks down— application. By helping corporate leaders develop a culture of true accountability, he has opened them to the possibility of much greater success.

David E. Wright (Wright)

Today, we're talking to Charles Davis, who is the president of Saga Worldwide. He works with CEOs and their executive teams and trains other consultants to do deeper-level work with executives. He is a past corporate CEO and was voted Business Leader of the Year in 1992. He has chaired two CEO and two Key Executive think tanks in the Washington, D.C., area. He has developed his own unique style of executive coaching, which concentrates on looking past the symptoms and digging down to the core issues. He has held many government positions in Gaithersburg, which is Maryland's second largest city, such as the charter chair of the Economic Development Committee, chairman of the 21st Century Committee, member of the board of appeals, city commissioner, and he was elected as city councilman and served as the council's vice-president. He also served as president of the Gaithersburg Chamber of Commerce. Mr. Davis, welcome to *Taking Charge.*

Charles Davis (Davis)

Thank you. It's good to be with you.

Wright

You've been a successful CEO, a successful councilman, successful in a number of senior executive positions throughout your career, but now you spend most of your time coaching CEOs and senior executives individually and in groups with Saga Worldwide's retreat programs. Looking at leadership issues from both sides, what do most executives struggle with in their quest for becoming better leaders?

Davis

That's an interesting question. I've had the opportunity to interview hundreds of CEOs in the course of my work. There is one thing that is very consistent. When we begin talking about some of their greatest fears and challenges, there's one that is consistent. Many of them state it this way, "One of my greatest fears is being found out." When we dig a little deeper into that, I usually get a story something like this. "I was working hard and working my way up through the organization, up the corporate ladder. Then one thing led to another, and one day I found myself CEO! I'm not quite sure how I got here, and now people presume that I have all the answers, but the truth is that I don't. My greatest fear is that my people are going to find out that I don't know everything." So it's an interesting place to begin working with a CEO, when they admit that they're afraid that people are going to find out that he's just a regular person, with fears and shortcomings just like everyone else.

Wright

Most of us imagine that CEOs had a goal-setting plan written on the wall in their bedroom with steps and ladders and visual aids and everything and worked their way up specifically to be the CEO. So it's interesting that you find that they just found themselves in charge and are not sure what to do with it.

Davis

It does appear to happen with great consistency. Even if they do work hard and plot their way to the top, once they finally reach that position they realize, "Uh-oh! The buck stops here. I must make the decisions. Am I really ready for this?"

Wright

What advice do you have for a leader who could engage these issues and accelerate his journey to the next level?

Davis

The more research we do around that question, the more we realize that the answer lies in ancient wisdom and not in the new management theorist's concepts. It's all built around the concept that unless you can kill the old beliefs that drive the behaviors and results you are not happy with, new beliefs that will drive different results can't really be instituted into the organization. So it's really about figuring out who we are as an executive team, who we want to be and what has to die for us to be able to close the gap.

Wright

Many consultants help companies create their values and mission statements in hopes of changing their people. They communicate these throughout the organization to address these issues and eliminate the problems of the past. Why not just do that? Wouldn't it be a lot easier?

Davis

Certainly that's a very popular approach. And really, there is nothing wrong with creating values and the mission statements; they can be valuable tools. But these don't address the real problems. The real problems are often driven underground, where they can continue and thrive. When you look at large-scale change programs, you'll find that the statistics are pretty miserable. You don't see in the consulting brochures the high failure rates that really take place; it's just overwhelming. Did you ever wonder why it is so rare that consultants offer a money-back guarantee on the results of their work? I believe that it is because they often come in and say, "What you need is a values statement and a mission statement, and then you get this word out to the people, then put up the posters in the lunch room, and the transformation will be underway." They don't offer a money-back guarantee, because this rarely has any lasting or measurable positive impact on an organization. What we've found that does work—and by the way, we do offer a money-back guarantee—is that if you can expose the real issues, get the truth on the table, the leaders and the organization can have a transformational experience. You know, once people are brave enough to tell the truth about the situation and about the organization, they can then address the real issues. Accountability will rise, passion for the success of the organization will rise and true, meaningful and lasting change can take place.

Wright

So you are saying that telling the truth is part of the secret. Why would they not be truthful if their very careers are on the line?

Davis

We often observe that the culture of an organization is built around not telling the truth. We've bumped into organizations where the people will tell us, "The boss does not want the truth or any bad news. Do not take bad news to the boss if you want to succeed around here." That kind of culture suppresses the real truth, and it's never addressed. Then one day, they wake up and realize that they are in a bad place and wonder how they got there. We were working with a 100-year-old company in Washington, D.C. We spent three days with them in an executive team retreat, and the current CEO said that as far as he knew, those three days were the first time in the history of that company that truth was actually put on the table and dealt with. That's an amazing thing when you think about the culture that would allow an organization to go for generations with telling the truth— and suffering the results of such behavior.

Wright

But if leaders take charge by challenging the status quo, isn't that dangerous? What if their superiors and subordinates don't follow them?

Davis

The real risk is not taking appropriate risk, not being brave enough to risk your career to really challenge the status quo. Otherwise, you continue to serve an emptiness and process that is not going to allow the company to succeed as it should. What's constantly missing in the case studies of the great failed companies is that these companies had read all of the latest books, they took all of the popular seminars, they hired all of the expert speakers and consultants, but they still failed. We realize that there are much deeper questions that the leaders are not asking. For example, what are we avoiding in this company, and why do we avoid it? What is broken around here that we're pretending is okay? What are we afraid to talk about? What are the things that are off limits in our corporate culture? Why don't we tell the truth to each other? Those are the deeper questions that will surface, the things that must be worked on to achieve excellence. In my experience as a CEO and working with hundreds of CEOs, CEOs really aren't looking for status-quo lemmings that will follow them off the cliff. They're looking for people who will tell them the truth, who will stand up for what they believe, who will take more risk and allow themselves to be held to a higher standard of accountability. The interesting thing is, employees are looking up at the leadership, and they want to see the exact same things. Yet there is so little of that going on in our corporations.

Wright

We mentioned mission statements in passing. What do you think about mission statements? Are they a good idea? Let me say why I ask the question. Everyone talks about change, you know; Toffler talked about it twenty years ago—not only change but rapid change. A mission statement seems to me to be an oxymoron in a corporation. What do you think?

Davis

People sometimes confuse mission statements and values statements, and as I said earlier, they can be good, they do have a place. They are good tools to capture your ideas and get them down in writing. But the problem we see is that until you first understand the beliefs that really drive what's going on in the organization, the mission statements and values statements are just empty words plastered on the wall. There must be alignment around the appropriate beliefs for an organization to begin to see people behaving differently. We go into organizations and we talk with CEOs who are just puzzled and frustrated. He or she will say to us, "I don't understand it. I sent out the memos about doing better customer service. I bought the customer service posters and put them on the lunch room wall. I had everyone read the new book on how to be a customer-driven company—and nothing has changed." Nothing has changed, because their beliefs about customer service have not changed. Until they have a new set of beliefs about customer service, they will continue to behave the same way and get the same results. So mission statements can be very useful tools, but they will not, in and of themselves, cause a behavioral change. Our premise is pretty simple; the results we get are driven by our behaviors, which will drive the results we get. So if we don't change our behavior, we will continue to get the same result. We really need to delve into what beliefs the corporation is holding onto and how they may or may not be appropriate for the future we say we want.

Wright

I remember a few years ago, I sat in a room with twenty or thirty church leaders. We were, among other things, trying to hammer out a mission statement. I mean, we inspected every word, because we might put it on the bulletin or hang it in the church somewhere. We wanted to have it fit exactly what we were doing. It occurred to me that there is a passage in our Bible that says, "Go ye therefore..."—the Great Commission—and I'm wondering why we didn't just make a copy of it and hang it up? I mean, it took us half a day, and finally, when I said that, everyone looked at me like I was stupid.

Davis

We certainly agree that simple truth is better. I believe it is West Point, as I recall, where their entire code to live by goes something like "Don't lie, cheat or steal or tolerate anyone who does." That says all that needs to be said. They live by it, and they make all of their decisions based on it.

Wright

I grew up near a large plant—they were a mill and mine company—and I can remember to this day, 50 or 60 years later, the tagline on their sign. It was simply, "Keep the mine running." And I thought, "That says a lot about keeping your employees employed."

Davis

That really pretty much says all that needs to be said, doesn't it?

Wright

How does one go about creating a strong team to ensure that a company's vision and values are honored?

Davis

This is going to sound kind of simple and old-fashioned, but if you think about it it's simply *by example*. The example that leadership portrays is really driven by what people observe when watching their behavior. It's not what they say or what they plaster on the wall that matters; it is their example. The leadership team needs to commit to the journey of killing the beast that holds them in the past in order to give birth to an appropriate future. You know the things that keep us in that past: "But it's tradition. It's the way we've always done it." It's the fear of changing. It's this problem of not dealing with real truth and pretending that it's something else.

Frankly, it's just not being able to make the appropriate decisions and make them fast enough. That's what leaders are for. It's the main job of a leader to be the inspiring and appropriate example for those they lead. We were talking about the values and mission. They have to become part of the culture of the new organization and not just printed, posted and forgotten about. Making these things real in a daily way by living them will change the beliefs of the people and, consequently, change their behavior.

We have found that an ancient tool for helping everyone stay on track is a behavioral code of honor—first for the leadership and then for the rest of the organization. It's really a code of how we're going to function with each other; how we're going to work together. It's about honoring and respecting each other and caring about each other enough to tell the truth. It is a way to establish a very high level of accountability. When we talk to CEOs and get around to that accountability question, they often appear to be ashamed when they have to say, "We really don't have much in the way of accountability around here, at any level."

Wright

As you highlight accountability, and especially the examples of an old-fashioned and better way, I would tend to agree. Do you find it odd, then, that with all of these problems that we've had in the recent past with voracity in companies and that sort of thing, that the CEOs in many cases took five- to fifteen-million-dollar packages while their companies were going down the tubes?

Davis

That's a really interesting thing to think about. Another ancient concept that can get into an organization and wreak havoc is just plain old greed. Perhaps a lot of what took place was driven by that mysterious part of us that we call ego. The answer is for all of us as leaders to work at pushing down our egos and allowing ourselves to be more vulnerable. In fact, I believe that leaders will be more powerful and be better leaders the more comfortable they get with being uncomfortable. When our egos rise up and we can't make an honorable decision, we see things happen like you were describing.

Wright

Someone told me in an interview recently, in a book about management, that in his opinion, the difference between a leader and a manager was vision. Would you agree with that?

Davis

Certainly. I think that is absolutely true. Someone else said that managers are about creating order and planning and executing it in an orderly fashion and that leaders are about disrupting order, because in order for the organization to grow, there has to be change, and change is a disruption to the order that managers are trying to keep. Managers want order, and that's what we want them to be doing, and leaders are about disrupting that order and finding bigger, better and more productive ways to do things.

Wright

That's a great thought. The man that I just referenced said it a different way. He said, "Leaders think that if it ain't broke, fix it anyway."

Davis

I like that a lot. I have been accused of thinking that way many times. That's what leaders are for. But what we find when we study organizations is that that is not the role that leaders are playing. Leaders often play the role of trying to keep order, and because of that, their companies can become stale and stagnant, because they are not creating the necessary change to be leaders in their industry. And then leaders sit in meetings and wring their hands wondering why they're not growing and achieving their goals. So leaders need to create a little disorder or "fix it even if it ain't broke" once in a while.

Wright

With our *Taking Charge* book, we're trying to encourage people in our audience, our readers, to be better, to live better and be more fulfilled by listening to the examples of our guests. Is there anyone in your life who has made a difference for you and helped you to become a better person?

Davis

I have been very, very fortunate in my life to have had many great mentors. When you ask that question, one that pops to mind is a gentleman named Morris Shechtman. I spent a great deal of time with him in the mountains of Montana. He wrote the book *Working Without a Net and The*

Internal Frontier. He helped me understand how important it is for a leader to do deep personal work with himself in order to be a better leader. Knowing oneself and coming to terms with who we are and what drives us will allow us to be more vulnerable and use our creative energy in a positive way. I learned through his tutelage that we'll become better leaders, as I said before, when we get more comfortable with allowing ourselves to be uncomfortable. That's a very hard thing for the top people in organizations to do.

Wright

What a great title, *Working Without a Net*.

Davis

It is, and you know, Western culture doesn't teach us to do that very well. We all want a safety line, and the truth is that most great or meaningful things happen on the edge, where it's not so safe. Great leaders understand that and allow themselves to be vulnerable. We all know that surviving the tough times really teaches us and prepares us for the future. As I spent time with Mr. Shechtman, I did a lot of deep personal work. It helped me to understand leadership and, I believe, help me to be more effective as I attempt to assist others with their leadership skills and mindset.

Wright

So what you're doing now with Saga Worldwide is working with individuals to build them into better leaders, with a belief system that can support the kind of organization they say they want. This must change not only their companies but also their lives.

Davis

Absolutely. We often get calls from CEOs that go something like this: "I was playing golf with one of my buddies who was always miserable and complaining about his company and its lack of productivity. Then he engaged Saga Worldwide, and now he's a happy guy. So I want some of that. I want you to come to my company and fix my people." We always say, "Wow. We wish we had the power to fix your people, or anyone else for that matter, but that's really not within our capabilities. But what we can do is come over and talk with you, the CEO, and your leadership team about dealing with the truth in your organization and getting into greater alignment. You must truly become the leaders that it will take to make your organization great." The thing that they struggle with, that is so difficult for them to think about as CEOs and leaders, is the concept that "It may not be them; it may be me who needs to adjust and change." Once the CEO and the leadership team understand that most of the trouble in their company starts with them, then they can start a journey of adjusting the organization and modifying it so it can move forward. The people will then have leaders that they are willing to follow. We typically start our work with the CEO, then with the entire executive team and finally help them move forward with taking it down into their organization.

Wright

Reflecting on the gentleman who was your mentor, what do you think makes up a great mentor? In other words, are there characteristics that mentors seem to have in common?

Davis

My experience indicates that they do have characteristics in common. The last thing that we need in this world is another guru who thinks that he has all of the answers. But great mentors, I believe, have done good, solid work with themselves, and they've come to terms with their own shortcomings and what they need to work on. Good mentors have seen bad times and survived them, and they take those experiences and learn from them. They have a love for sharing lessons, these life lessons, with other people. I teach a class several times a year on how to be a mentor. A huge piece of mentoring is understanding that adults don't learn through download. Adults learn through the process of discovery and experiencing things. They must discover the answer for themselves. A good mentor understands this and allows the student to learn by finding the answer for him or herself. Giving them the answer only gives them more information and solutions to choose from, and goodness knows they have enough information already. If information was going to save the world, it would already be saved, I suppose. But it's not about that. There are already too many choices. It's not a lack of information; it's that people have to discover the answers for themselves and then apply that answer as their solution. I think good mentors understand that and don't do download but coach and help a person find the answer.

Wright

I've done a lot of thinking about that word, "coach." A lot of people whom I work with and have worked with in the past are coaches. I can remember going back to junior high school—you know, in the seventh, eighth and ninth grades—there was a coach there who was every boy's mentor, because everyone loved him so much. After I grew up and got to my 40s and 50s, when he was a really old man, I still called him "coach." It was almost a reverent term as far as I was concerned.

Davis

What a wonderful thing. What do you think made him a good coach? What caused him to have such an impression on your life? What was it about him?

Wright

There were a lot of things. When I talked to him, he stopped everything he was doing and looked me straight in the eye. He was just a fine man. He was honest and above board, and he helped me. I came from rather meager beginnings, and he helped me make decisions and do the right things down through my life.

Davis

I think what you're also pointing out is that there was a huge level of trust that developed between the two of you. I think that's such a critical element when you're talking about coaching or consulting work, especially when working with CEOs. It's about developing that level of trust where they know that you have their best interests at heart and that you're going to be honest and tough. Quite frankly, something that consultants have a really hard time doing is being vulnerable. Being able to say, "I don't know," and not feel that it is okay not to know. The trust that developed between you two is exactly what's required for a great mentoring relationship.

Wright

He was an athletic coach, but I was not an athlete, so it didn't matter to him whether I played sports or not. What mattered was that I was a person. He really helped me a lot.

Davis

So he was really an effective and dedicated coach of young men and not just a sports coach. What a wonderful way to be remembered.

Wright

When you consider the choices that you have made down through the years, has faith played an important role in your life?

Davis

Absolutely. I believe that acknowledging the spiritual element in our lives is really critical for being well balanced and making sense of our place and our purpose in life. I think it's essential to our greater happiness. I meet a lot of leaders who have not allowed this facet to develop, and there's a noticeable gap. There's a noticeable hole there. A lot of leaders actually suffer from this, and they talk about it. It's an amazing thing to see. When I hear CEOs say that life is only about succeeding in business and making money, and then I'll often ask them the question, "Okay, if that's true, how will you know when you have enough? How much will be enough?" Then they'll think about it a while, and it is evident that they haven't spent much time thinking about this question before. They'll think for a while, and then they'll finally say, "Well, the truth is I probably already have enough." Then they almost always follow that with, "But if life's not about getting more, what is it about?" And that's the question that they need to ponder. When they allow themselves to search for that spiritual element, they often fill that void with very meaningful things. In Western culture, we do tend to measure everything in dollars, and I believe that there is much, much more to life. In my life, faith has been a key element in broadening my understanding of people and finding a life work and purpose. I believe that as a result of my faith, I've come to understand this about myself: I believe that I'm here on this earth to help others find out more about who they are and what their purpose is, and in doing so, I find out more about who I am and what my purpose is. So faith has played a very important part in my life.

Wright

One person put it pretty well in perspective for me one day a few years ago when we were talking about that very subject of wealth and how much is enough. He said, "You might want to look the next time a funeral procession comes by. You'll note that the second car never has a U-Haul attached." So I guess life must be about something else.

Davis

I agree. There is so much we might miss if we don't slow down and ask the important questions.

Wright

If you could have a platform and tell our readers something that you feel would help or encourage them, what would you say?

Davis

I would want them to realize, as I realize, that all of the results we're going to get in life are really driven by the way we behave. The way we behave is always driven by what we believe. You know, if we want to get a different result, we really need to come to terms with our beliefs and perhaps alter some of them a bit, which will change our behavior. So it makes no sense to keep behaving the same way over and over and expect to get a different result. In fact, I had a psychologist friend of mine tell me one time that that is one of the clinical definitions of insanity, to keep doing the same thing over and over and expecting something different to happen. Perhaps we need to change our behavior. So I'd encourage them to spend some time exploring what beliefs are really driving them. What beliefs may have to die in order for them to move to the next level? What are those beliefs based on? What adjustments do they want to make to ensure a different result?

Wright

What a great conversation. I really appreciate your talking to us this morning. You've given me a lot to ponder.

Today we have been talking to Charlie Davis, an award-winning business leader who is president of Saga Worldwide, LLC and, as we have found this morning, a very generous man with his time. Thank you so much, Charlie, for being with us today.

Davis

Thank you, David. It's been a pleasure.

Charles F. Davis
430 Belle Grove Road
Gaithersburg, MD 20877
Phone: 301.330.9597
Fax: 301.977.3481
E-mail: charlie@sagaworldwide.com

Chapter 10

DR. CATHY TROWER

Dr. Cathy Trower provides consulting services to boards about governance matters, to businesses about strategy and teamwork, and to colleges and universities about personnel issues and faculty diversity. As a facilitator, Trower's specialty involves combining her knowledge of governance, strategic thinking and teamwork to create an experience for governing boards and corporate teams that translates into energy, action and a sustained commitment to excellence.

David E. Wright (Wright)

Today, we're talking to Dr. Cathy Trower. She is Saga Worldwide's board governance expert as well as a consultant and facilitator for corporate executive retreat experiences. Nationally known for her work at Harvard University on faculty diversity, faculty employment policies and practices, governance and senior management issues, she can be found presenting her controversial insights at conferences around the country. As senior researcher and principal investigator at Harvard, she has edited a book and authored many articles. Her combined knowledge of governance, strategic planning and teamwork is invaluable for creating peak experiences for developing accountability, energy and action for governing boards and corporate teams. Ms. Trower, welcome to *Taking Charge.*

Dr. Cathy Trower (Trower)

Thank you.

Wright

I was interested in your work with Saga Worldwide in improving board and executive performance. You're currently based at Harvard University, where you publish and speak nationally on faculty employment issues. You also work on governance, especially of non-profit organizations. From your experience, what have you found frustrates many boards about the organizations they govern?

Trower

For non-profit organizations, colleges and universities, a major frustration is the lack of a bottom line; that is, a perceived lack of accountability and inability to hold the executive team accountable. Most board members come from the corporate sector and find this a bit frustrating. A second annoyance would be ambiguity, a lack of clarity around strategies, goals and priorities. Again, these concepts are much a daily part of the corporate sector, so board members often find themselves frustrated when they sit on boards of non-profits or colleges and universities. A third aggravation would be internal politics like power and control issues. It's not to say that these don't exist in the for-profit world, but as board members, they may see the political ploys as somewhat frivolous and petty in the non-profit setting. A fourth frustration is the lack of clarity around roles and responsibilities. There tends to be some confusion around the roles and responsibilities of board members as well as the boundaries between directors/trustees and the executive team. Another irritation would be trying to interpret and understand the CEO's expectations for board performance of the board as a whole as well as individual directors/trustees. Oftentimes, those expectations are unclear. A final frustration that we've seen is the lack of red meat, or substance, on the table. This can cause a board to feel like a rubber stamp.

Wright

Are most of these board positions voluntary positions?

Trower

Yes.

Wright

So they're not getting paid?

Trower

Correct.

Wright

That would be real problem, wouldn't it?

Trower

It's a big difference from those who sit on corporate boards. Non-profit board members are volunteering their time and thus hope that board meetings would be a good use of their time. I think it does raise the bar on that expectation. In many cases, trustees are expected to make charitable donations to the organization. They pay for the privilege of being on the board! Their time should be well spent since it is not well compensated.

Wright

I've had experience sitting on boards before. I remember when I had about five companies going at one time, all of them very profitable. It took really tight management. I had five or six people sitting on my board who were all getting paid great salaries because they were a part of the organization. When I sat on the volunteer boards, it used to frustrate me, because I would want to make business kinds of decisions, and the other people would either not be equipped to do that or wouldn't want to do it.

Trower

That's a huge issue, especially when the composition of the board is quite diverse. There may be some people around the table who are alumni of the institutions or, in the case of a school, a parent of an enrolled student. Some may have no background or experience as a trustee or as a decision maker. In still other cases, they are on the board because they have a lot of money and they are a potential donor. Still others are corporate executives who volunteer their time and talents to a non-profit organization out of a sense of civic duty. Therefore, it is not uncommon to have a very diverse group of people sitting around the table, and I do think this presents a challenge.

Wright

On the flip side of the coin, in your experience, what frustrates executive leaders about boards?

Trower

The first one is the flip side of the same coin, in this case, holding the board accountable. It's a bit like your point about a diverse board. If they're volunteers, a CEO has to wonder how accountable they can be. That's a big frustration. The second one would be that either it's a huddle of quarterbacks or everyone is sidelined. In some cases, you have a whole bunch of people who want to call the shots, or you have a lot of people who are sitting it out and are just there for other reasons and not always knowing why. A third frustration is that they meet a couple of times a year, so the board lacks cohesiveness. Therefore, what is on the table oftentimes seems like it's a waste of time, because there's no way to cover really substantive issues when they meet so rarely and with large periods of time in between. Oftentimes, thus, the board becomes a rubber stamp. Board members report on the minutes of various committee meetings. It's mostly about information sharing than decision making.

Wright

I understand that the work that you do at Saga takes boards and senior executives on a journey to address these types of issues, but you've been more successful by avoiding the use of standard consulting techniques or popular leadership theories. So how do you do it?

Trower

Most of the methods that we use at Saga are based on techniques that have been used by leaders for thousands of years but for some reason aren't in practice today. In fact, most of the popular theories today have not only failed to create great leaders but they've generated really fertile ground for *Dilbert*™, the cartoon, and a great deal of cynicism. We find that powerful results happen when we get people to reveal their underlying belief patterns that generate the undesirable behavior that they complain about. In other words, everybody can see it. They know what's going on, but nobody wants to talk about it. Once you get them to reveal those underlying belief patterns, they see that the world in which they're working was jaded and that that world exists because they created it that way. The beauty of that, then, is to take them through some experiences that show them that if they confront reality with the things they think but won't say, they can create a new future. So it's that path forward, that future that can be created, but there is a cost involved. It can be a painful process.

Wright

In the work that you do at Saga, you've discovered that the journey of leadership is not necessarily a fun or even a motivational experience. In fact, as you just mentioned, there is a serious cost factor. Could you tell me about this?

Trower

The cost is on the personal side. In fact, we refer to it as suicide. So yes, it's pretty painful! It's pretty ugly. Who would want to hire us to commit suicide? But the idea is that it's the death of the ego, not the actual person. This takes us back to the ancient executives—the samurai—who knew that unless they killed the old beliefs, the new ones could not be instituted into a civilization. A big part of the journey is, therefore, understanding what has to die and being committed to taking that journey. It's definitely not for the faint-hearted, but that's where real accountability begins to emerge. You can confront your own ego and kill it and say, "I realize how my own ego is stopping this organization or executive team or board from achieving high performance." That's where the power comes in.

Wright

So this is different from the "program-of-the-month" services that many boards and managers complain about?

Trower

Definitely. It's like nothing most people have ever experienced.

Wright

How do you overcome the cynicism for leadership development programs that exists in many companies today?

Trower

That's a great question. We actually don't. We bring cynicism to the table. The way we do that is we figure that people are too smart to be conned with the motivational posters and the coffee mugs and what we consider to be pretty shallow training exercises. Most people have seen hundreds of consultants and lots of trainers, and we find that it is always better to tell the truth. We don't condescend to the people we work with. We don't just put out another set of cheesy platitudes. Ironically, when people enter an authentic journey of leadership, a lot of them cry for more of the touchy-feely stuff, the gentler stuff. Real leadership can be painful, because we have to shine the light into our inner selves and confront those dark places that most of us would rather hide. We've gotten pretty good at hiding it from ourselves, and we've gotten really good at hiding that from others. So we make sure that the client is ready before we accept them as a client. This is really necessary, because we are probably the only management consulting group that guarantees results with a money-back offer. Because we only use methods proven to have worked over a thousand years, we're really confident in what we do.

Wright

I found out many, many years ago that leadership is painful and it's personally painful. For me, I had 175 people working for me one time, and I envisioned myself as this great leader and community leader. The truth of the matter was I had an open-door policy. I just sat there and listened all day long and sometimes got my heart broken with all of the problems that my people were having—daughters that were pregnant, sons that were doing strange things, all kinds of problems. It seemed to be the answer. By just listening and not really doing anything about it, they thought I was very intelligent.

Trower

Good for you!

Wright

What do you tell managers and leaders who are uncertain that their current team is sufficient to win tomorrow's challenge?

Trower

First, we ask them if they're willing to lose people. If the leaders in the organization are weak, it's difficult for the followers to follow. If the leaders are not brave enough to step up to that, then there's an even deeper problem. Some boards have a hard time confronting weak CEOs. A lot of times it's a "good old boys" club, and that's clear to everyone in the organization except the board. This works the other way, too. Sometimes, it's very difficult for a CEO to confront a board chair's weaknesses even though everyone else knows what they are. That's really the first question: Are you willing to lose people? That's oftentimes a very difficult question to answer, but it's really crucial to us being able to work with the organization.

Wright

You mean lose people at the top or at the bottom?

Trower

I mean lose people at the top. We're talking about the executive team. Those people, or board members, might not make it through this journey. So yes, are you willing to risk that? What we found is if the leadership team—executive management—can't make it, how can we expect anyone else in the organization to make it? It's a challenge.

Wright

That's a tough one. To lose people at the bottom is easy. To lose them at the top is another question. So how does one go about creating a strong board to ensure great leadership will occur in the organization?

Trower

We feel that it helps when the board or executive team is constituted with people whose beliefs are aligned; otherwise, their fragmentation can spill over into the organization. In fact, we find belief misalignment the most common denominator in weak boards and in weak executive teams. I'm not talking about views here. I just want to make that distinction. There's a difference between views and belief alignment. A variety of viewpoints and opinions is very important, but beliefs drive behavior and behavior drives results. So aligned, shared beliefs are very important.

Wright

With this book, *Taking Charge*, one of our goals is to try to encourage people who are reading our book to be better, to live better and be more fulfilled by listening to the examples of our guests. Is there anything or anyone in your life who has made a difference for you and helped you to become a better person?

Trower

I've actually done a lot of thinking about that, and the most obvious answers for me are my parents, siblings, spouse, mentors, close friends and my teachers. But I'd like to answer the question another way. It may sound strange, but I have to say everyone. That is, I have learned something from everyone I encounter, and I guess, in my estimation, if you invite people to be honest with you about yourself, most of the time they are, and you learn something. So I'm constantly growing and learning and, I hope, getting better with my communication and interaction with others. My gut instinct is to trust others, and I think that helps. Sometimes it hurts, because people are honest with you, and it's not really what you want to hear. I think, especially if this is what we're going to go out and work with in executive teams and boards, we need to be able to walk the talk. I've really opened up my own personal life to doing that, and it's made a big difference.

Wright

As a teacher and leader, what do you think makes up a great mentor? You spoke of mentors a minute ago. In other words, are there characteristics that mentors seem to have in common?

Trower

I guess, for me, it would be the ability to meet people where they are and to kind of find out their triggers, then to either gently massage those or even use tougher tactics. That is, to bring out the best that a person has to offer. I think a third would be to listen carefully, and a fourth characteristic of a great mentor is to care deeply about the human condition.

Wright

Someone told me one time that some great mentors were like an oyster. They were always confronting you. When sand gets in an oyster, it makes a pearl, and only through irritation or confrontation do you really grow and become a pearl, which is a beautiful thing.

Trower

That's interesting. I really like that.

Wright

When I ask people to list the three people who were most influential in their lives, with the exception of their parents, I almost always hear that two out of the three, and sometimes all three, of these folks were teachers. I wonder if teachers really know how revered they are later on in life.

Trower

Right. We don't appreciate them at the time, necessarily! I'm fortunate in that a couple of my mentors were professors of mine. They were professors first, and then they've been mentors to me in my career. I even remember some grade school teachers, so I think you're absolutely right.

Wright

Most people are fascinated with these new television shows about being a survivor. What has been the greatest comeback that you've made from adversity in your career or in your life?

Trower

I guess it would have to be from in my life. There was a time when my self-esteem was very low and manifested itself in self-destructive behaviors, in poor relationships, smoking and drinking. I realized that I had choices to make. I could continue down that path, or I could take another, and I decided to take another. I feel very fortunate to have recognized that I had a choice and to see another path. I think that too often when self-esteem takes a blow, either from something terrible that happens or a rough period of time, people often don't see that there is a choice and that they can rise above it and get out of it. I really think, for me, it was having other people in my life that helped me see that.

Wright

These people who sit on these non-profit boards come into this relationship just as you have said. Some of them are broken by divorce or bad habits or by business failures and all of those kinds of things. Do those kinds of things manifest themselves in their actions or in the way they work on the boards?

Trower

I think they almost have to. Some people are a lot better at separating their personal lives from their professional lives. I know that when we've worked in a retreat experience, with executive teams especially, that it's a little easier to do with executive teams than with boards. I'll say why. Basically, an executive team is on their job eight, ten, twelve hours a day. It's pretty hard for them not to bring what's happening with them personally into the workplace and vice versa; they take their workplace back home with them. We have found that the more honest they are with each other about what they're going through personally, realizing how that could be affecting them on the job, as well as being honest at home about what's happening to them at work, the less destructive it all can be for them, because they find a support group. Not that work should be a support group but that once it's just out there, people can go, "I get it. You're going through a divorce. I didn't know that." You can separate yourself from it, and you can also empathize with the person. I do think that kind of honesty can be very helpful rather than bringing the baggage to bear without ever confronting it or saying that it's there.

Wright

When you work with these boards, do you do any personality profile like Myers-Briggs or DISC or any of those kinds of tools?

Trower

Yes. We actually do both. Saga does mostly the DISC now, but Myers-Briggs is another great one to use.

Wright

I started taking the DISC in 1973, and there's no way I can fool it. I just can't believe it. I thought surely I would have learned by now how to fool it.

Trower

I haven't been taking it for that many years. That's a great story. It is amazing. It really nails people. It's powerful stuff.

Wright

When you consider the choices you've made down through the years, has faith played an important role in your life?

Trower

Yes. Absolutely. I've always believed that there's a force that is greater than we are and is there to help guide us, and I think that force is love. For some it's a love of God, for others it's a love of humanity, but I just tend to think of it as love. It's interesting, because I was involved in a retreat experience with an executive team just about a week ago. What was fascinating in this all-male group was that love was one of the things that they actually listed as being very important in leadership. I was really amazed by that. For me, that's what it is. That's what faith is all about.

Wright

That was going to be my next question. Can you get away with talking about the touchy-feely subject with male-oriented boards?

Trower

With some, it's a little easier than with others. Some of them honestly have very little tolerance for what they consider to be parlor games or touchy-feely stuff. I think honestly, though, that when you drill down deep, we're all humans, and without that, there's not a whole lot there. I think most of it is that we put up our protective shields and we portray one thing on the outside that may have little to do with what's on the inside. But when you peel that all back and you get inside, people realize that that's what really matters.

Wright

I've heard many times that the second car in a funeral procession never has a U-Haul behind it. Since you can't take the material things with you, there's got to be something else. If you could have a platform and tell our readers something that you feel would help or encourage them, what would you say to them?

Trower

I guess just two things. Aim high and go for it. There's nothing you can't do or become.

Wright

Why do you think it is that people find that hard to believe, especially that you can basically become anything you want to become? I'm 5' 7", so I'll never play in the NBA. There are some physical limitations, but most of my friends and the people that I've known down through the years don't really believe that, that you can be anything you want to be in this country.

Trower

I don't know why. I wonder if they've really tried. I really believe in envisioning a future and the power of a vision. If you can't even see it or dream it, it certainly isn't going to happen, but if you can see it and dream it, there's got to be a pathway to it, and you have to just persevere and not give up. I've just seen too many people who have risen from the depths. They grew up in the ghetto; they grew up in the most awful conditions and have risen on to greatness as executives, as leaders, as athletes, as politicians. That's not to say it's not a lot easier for the people who were born into privilege, but that's a very few of us. I'm not sure why people don't believe it except maybe they just haven't tried hard enough or they haven't tried more than one route. If you really have your heart set on something, and one pathway didn't get you there, try another pathway.

Wright

I always thought that Olympic winners were born with the ability and everything. What's fascinating to me when I read about the Olympics—which would be my way of looking at success, because that's about as far as you can go—one thing that strikes me really strangely is that the difference between winning and losing is not seconds, but milliseconds. The rewards for winning are like a thousand times more than one for coming in second, but they beat them by a breath, and that's what's fascinating. Another thing is that some of these great winners were crippled, they had emphysema, and they came through devastating illnesses to become Olympic winners. It's unbelievable.

Trower

I know; isn't that amazing? Every time I don't feel like getting on my treadmill to run, I picture someone in a wheelchair. I say to myself, "What is your problem?" You see these people, like you said, who are missing limbs and they're skiing or they're blind. So we have no excuse. As you said, you may not play pro basketball, but there are other things you can do.

Wright

We have been talking today to Dr. Cathy Trower, who is affiliated with Saga Worldwide. She's a consultant and a facilitator for corporate executive retreats and experiences. Thank you so much for being with us today. I really enjoyed it.

Trower

Fantastic. Thank you so much.

Dr. Cathy Trower
Saga Worldwide, Inc.
135 Mountain Rd.
Weare, NH 03281
Phone: 410.528.0800
Email: cathy_trower@gse.Harvard.edu
Web: www.sagaworldwide.com

Chapter 11

DEBORAH EVANS COX
& ED HENDRICKS

Deborah Evans Cox is a founding partner of IgniteSpirit, LLC and has particular hands-on expertise in the fields of leadership development, personal growth, team building, diversity, spirituality in the workplace, organizational growth and development, interpersonal communication skills, managing conflict and relationship building. She has more than twenty years of management and leadership experience working in major corporations such as D&B Computing Services, Xerox and Pitney Bowes, in  *such areas as training, diversity, change management, customer services, human resources, information systems, technical consulting and sales support. She is the author of numerous articles on various aspects of leadership and serves as a personal and professional coach to corporate CEOs and other individuals.*

Ed Hendricks is a co-founding partner of IgniteSpirit, a certified association executive, a certified management consultant, a professional member of the National Speakers Association, an entrepreneur, a university professor and a former CEO of a major international trade organization. He has served as director of the Leadership Studies Program and director of the Center for Corporate Education at Sacred Heart University in Connecticut. Ed is listed in Who's Who in America, Who's Who in the World *and has been selected as one of the Outstanding Individuals of the 20th Century. He has appeared on* CNN International *and on* CBS television *as well as in* The New York Times *and* The Wall Street Journal. *Ed is the author of three books on consulting, business networking and living a full life, and he is a contributing author in three other books on relationship marketing, consulting and leadership.*

David E. Wright (Wright)

Today, we are talking with the founding partners of IgniteSpirit, LLC, Edward D. Hendricks and Deborah Evans Cox. Ed was president and CEO of an international trade organization and has been serving as director of the Center for Corporate Education and director of the Leadership Studies program at Sacred Heart University in Fairfield, Connecticut. Deborah has been an executive at Fortune 500 companies, including Xerox, Pitney Bowes and Dun & Bradstreet. She brings to the table professional expertise in the fields of leadership development, management skills, change management, personal growth, team building, diversity and spirituality. Deborah and Ed, welcome to *Taking Charge.*

Edward Hendricks (Hendricks)

Thank you, Dave.

Deborah Evans Cox (Cox)

Thank you.

Wright

Both of you say that leaders require a combination of intelligence, emotional maturity and spirituality. What are some of the components that go into your leadership equation?

Hendricks

We devised an equation that basically says that leadership equals I.Q. plus E.Q. plus S.Q. What we mean by that is to be a leader today requires a combination of intelligence, emotional maturity and spirituality. Traditionally, intelligence quotients have been concerned with such things as logical reasoning, task skills, general knowledge, the ability to see analogies and identifying relationships among concepts or things. The I.Q. test has traditionally been used to measure verbal reasoning, abstract visual reasoning and other reasoning skills. We believe that is no longer enough. It is no longer sufficient to be high in intelligence and to have good technical skills. Some of the soft skills, as they are often called, are more important today in making a successful leader than they have been in the past. The emotional quotient, or E.Q., includes such things as self-awareness, self-management, empathy, social skills and the ability to influence others as well as to motivate oneself. Spiritual quotient, S.Q., involves our realization that there is something outside of and larger than ourselves and even larger than the companies we might represent. S.Q. looks for connectedness with others that goes beyond empathy to a realization that we really are, in some way, all part of a greater whole. It applies to looking at such things as purpose, meaning, ethics and values. In short, I.Q. primarily solves logical problems. E.Q. allows us to judge situations that we're in and then to behave appropriately. S.Q. helps us look at the deeper qualities of the situation and the connection between ourselves and others as well as the connection and impact we may have on the immediate and related situation.

Wright

So I.Q. has reasoning factored into the equation?

Hendricks

I.Q. primarily plays the role of determining a person's ability to reason quantitatively. I.Q. does not consider such things as social or emotional intelligence. We agree with Daniel Goleman who says that it is four times more important to being a good leader to have emotional intelligence and a high emotional quotient than to have just a high I.Q. As he points out, no matter what leaders set out to do, their success depends on how they do it.

Wright

E.Q. has received a lot of attention since Daniel Goleman's books *Emotional Intelligence* and *Primal Leadership*. In what ways does the E.Q. of a leader impact followers and an organization?

Cox

First, let's talk about what E.Q. means. Emotional intelligence has been defined as "an array of emotional, personal, social abilities and skills that influence one's ability to succeed in coping with the environment." Dr. Ruben Barone, John Mayer and Peter Sullivan have described it as "the ability to monitor one's own and others' feelings and emotions and to discriminate among them and use this information to guide one's thinking and actions." E.Q. was originally coined by a clinical psychologist; then in the mid-1990s, Daniel Goleman revealed findings in neuroscience and psychology that stressed the importance of emotional quotient. E.Q. makes us aware of our feelings and the feelings of others. Goleman identifies five categories of emotional intelligence: self-awareness, self-management, social skills, personal influence and empathy toward others. The Emotional quotient, involves empathy, motivation, compassion and the ability to respond to pleasure, external and internal pressure, and pain. It is through the effective functioning of these areas that we are able to think effectively, learn, solve problems, make better decisions, behave appropriately, remember and build and maintain relationships, thereby impacting others. Emotional intelligence provides us with the ability to manage ourselves and our relationships appropriately.

Wright

One of your popular workshops is Effective Communication Skills. Does this tie to the question of leadership?

Cox

Yes; very much so. In our workshops, we talk about the importance of building relationships with the people with whom you work, including those inside your organization as well as with your customers, your suppliers and your stakeholders. Empathy is a key to building good relationships. First and foremost is the ability to truly listen to others. Listening actively and fully to someone and putting our own inner voices aside helps us to understand what is really going on with the other person. From that, we build empathy. When we can understand the feelings and emotions of the other person, we can then respond in an appropriate manner. Recognizing our own emotions and learning to understand and manage them is also essential to effective leadership. In our communications skills program, we use a process called Dialogue that requires listening actively, respecting differences, suspending our own position and focusing on learning rather than making assumptions. There are five key components of effective Dialogue. The first is suspension. We suspend our preliminary thoughts and reactions, our former experiences and our assumptions about a person or the subject. The second is identifying assumptions. We look at our beliefs and opinions about how things should be or how the world works. Suspending and identifying assumptions enables us to more clearly look at what's really happening; what really is the information that we are receiving in a communication. This is a challenge for most of us. We naturally prejudge, fill in the gaps of unknown information and make assumptions based on prior experiences and knowledge about the person with whom we are speaking or the subject we are talking about. When we are able to suspend our thoughts and opinions, we become more open to listening, learning and allowing ourselves to engage in a new experience of the person or the situation. The third component of dialogue is active listening, whereby we listen for meaning and inquire about what the person is experiencing, feeling and trying to express. We also examine the meaning behind our own words, thoughts and emotions. The fourth component involves balancing our own thoughts and opinions with asking the other person for his or her ideas and feelings. This balanced give-and-take allows us to learn from one another. The fifth component is reflection. Taking time to reflect and make sense of the multifaceted picture helps us move forward in a collaborative and generative manner. As we deliberately suspend, inquire, reflect and understand, we are better able to mange emotions that may be stirring. Further, we open ourselves to learning. We engender a collaborative environment. We create connections and deeper relationships. We are able to collaborate to create positive results. For leaders, effective communication, collaboration and strong relationships are key components of their effectiveness in their ability to lead.

Wright

You've also had firsthand experience in the area of diversity excellence. How might this fit into the leadership equation?

Cox

Effective leaders understand the value of differences, and they understand the magnitude of difference around us. Diversity is not only found in the obvious race and gender arena but it's also the idea that each of us comes to the table with different experiences, cultures, skills, ways of processing, beliefs, values, learning styles, personalities and needs. Taking all of that into account, it behooves leaders to learn about a person's uniqueness, value them and be able to adjust, respond, collaborate, motivate and work according to different styles and needs. Understanding, appreciating and leveraging the uniqueness of employees, colleagues, customers and stakeholders can determine how effectively the leader can tap into new ideas and lead the organization to positive change and desired results

Wright

In the introduction to the book *Successful Business Networking*, you claim that it's not what you know but whom you know that determines how far you will go. That certainly is true of leaders as well. Are there things people can do to make themselves more attractive to others so that other people will want to help them succeed?

Hendricks

In the book *Successful Business Networking* I start out with the adage that if you want to really succeed as a networker or as a leader, you're going to have to first be a giver. I believe that, for the most part, what determines how far you'll go in life is the people around you. The way to attract people can probably be summed up best by the simple prayer of St. Francis:

> *Lord, make me an instrument of your peace. Where there is hatred, let me sow love. Where there is injury, pardon. Where there is doubt, faith. Where there is despair, hope. Where there is darkness, light. Where there is sadness, joy. Oh, grant that I may not so much seek to be consoled as to console; to be understood as to understand; to be loved as to love. For it is in giving that we receive. It is in pardoning that we are pardoned, and it is in dying that we are born to eternal life.*

Think for a moment about how attractive someone would be to others if he or she were seen as a peacemaker and a bridge builder. How magnetic he would be if that person loved people and every place he went, rather than disseminating hatred or looking at people of different cultures, races or gender in a negative way, he really honored others for their differences. Suppose she went around pardoning people rather than harboring injury or holding onto bad feelings? People are also attracted to people who have conviction and self-confidence. So where there is doubt, the leader can instill faith by being a self-confident person. When people are in despair, the leader can envision a sense of hope by sharing a vision that the world will get better, that business can be better and the conditions can be better. If we take that simple prayer of St. Francis and apply it to ourselves, we can see how we can become much more attractive as individuals and certainly much more attractive as leaders by the simple message that he gave us.

Wright

In the book *The Insider's Guide to Consulting Success*, you identify ten keys for reducing stress. I'm sure all leaders, regardless of their profession or industry, suffer from a lot of stress. What are the keys to reducing stress as you see them?

Hendricks

I'd like to just enumerate the ten points, because I think that they are very valuable to leaders at all levels and to all individuals, as a matter of fact. Number one is taking yourself on a trip into the future. Think of yourself as you would like to be remembered in your eulogy, and then decide to become that kind of person. Keep that image in mind, and act in your life at all times as if you were that kind of person that that eulogy was being written about. Second, give yourself a daily pep talk to develop the habit of thinking about yourself positively. Get up in the morning and look in the mirror and, instead of looking for wrinkles and hair loss, look in the mirror and tell yourself what a great person you are and what a great day you can allow yourself to have. Three, make a list of the successes you have had in the past. Keep this list in a notebook and review and update the list frequently. It's amazing how hard it is for some people to identify successes that they've had in their lives or things that people like about them. It helps us to reduce stress when we remember that we do have a lot going for us. If we simply take the time to understand all of the successful things we have done in our lives, all of the things people like about us and all of the skills and attributes we have picked up along the way, our lives would be so much richer.

Number four is to avoid negative influences and to avoid negative people who pull you down. Don't hang around with people who drag you down all the time. Number five, get out of your comfort zone or your lazy zone by daring to do something that you might even fear doing. A way to reduce stress, believe it or not, is by getting out of where you presently are and looking for new opportunities. Number six is doing the best you can in any situation. Don't fool yourself into thinking you have to be perfect; you can't. As Salvador Dali, the artist, put it, "Don't worry about perfection; you'll never achieve it." Number seven, forgive yourself for making mistakes and appreciate your accomplishments. Here's a tip: Treat yourself as you would treat your best friend. Number eight, have faith in your own judgment and your ability to make good decisions. You're a lot brighter, a lot smarter and a lot more of a leader than you give yourself credit for being. Number nine, learn to say no. Say no to demands that drain your time and your energy. Number ten, act. Achievements are the results of doing, not dreaming. Actively strive to become the kind of person you want to be. Focusing on what you want to be and living as if you were that person is a great way to reduce the stress of everyday life.

Wright

What can a leader do to increase his or her E.Q.?

Hendricks

I think that there are a number of things that a leader can do. In the book *Primal Leadership*, Daniel Goleman talks about some things that can be done. Some of the things that he talks about have to do with getting in touch with who you really are and identifying what people think about you and the skills that you have. Ask your peers, your supervisors and your subordinates all to do an evaluation of the skills that you have. The second step involves getting in touch with your ideal self and doing some introspection, meditation perhaps, on what and how you really want to be. Step three combines what you really want and how you would like to be and then developing what Goleman calls "a learning agenda," which is a plan to build on the strengths that you have and to reduce the gaps. Step four is to reconfigure your brain. Think about professional athletes who engage in visualization. They spend much more time visualizing what they're going to do on the golf course or on the basketball court or soccer field than they do actually playing in a game. Then they also practice a lot. To emotionally grow also requires practice. For example, practice taking time to step back rather than reacting immediately. Finally, step five talks about the power of relationships. To grow emotionally requires one to develop relationships and to develop a support system. Have people around you who are not "yes" men and "yes" women but people who can really assess your skills and attributes and help you to grow in those areas and who then foster that growth by supporting you and encouraging you along the way.

Wright

In one of your articles, and in some of your presentations, you talk about your belief that attitude, more than aptitude, equals altitude. What do you mean by that?

Hendricks

That goes back to our belief that intelligence and even technical skills are no longer sufficient to really rise within an organization, to become a leader, to develop as a CEO. Leadership success is dependent more on your attitude, how you relate with others, your emotional quotient and your spiritual quotient. For example, the Center for Creative Leadership took a look at what they called "derailed executives," which they identified as people who were rising stars but who somewhere along the way to the top flamed out. The Center's research identified that the reasons executives fail have to do with the following conditions: One was poor working relationships. Derailed executives did not have good relationships with the people with whom they worked. Another reason for failure was that they were seen as being very authoritarian. Another was that they were described as being overly ambitious. Another reason for flaming out was a conflict with top management. None of the reasons for getting derailed had anything to do with a lack of intelligence or poor technical skills. They were more what might be called emotional quotient reasons, and these have to do much more with attitude than with intelligence. So I believe truly that attitude more than aptitude equals altitude.

Wright

You mention spirituality as a key component for successful leadership. Spirituality seems to be a fairly new item in this context. Why do you think there is new interest in spirituality?

Cox

I'd like to start with the question, "What is spirituality?" There are probably as many definitions of spirituality as there are colors of crayons. Our definition for this conversation is that spirituality is a sense of self-awareness and a connection with and the honoring of all other people as well as a connection to something larger than ourselves. It may be expressed through acts of love, kindness, compassion, inner and external awareness, appreciation, and intimate relationships with one's own self and others. Spirituality allows us to ask the existential questions such as, "Why am I here? Who am I? What should I do? What do I stand for? What's my purpose in life? How do I fit into this world?" It requires a person to become more deeply introspective, to search for ways to express who he or she really is. Spirituality is about finding meaning, value and purpose and understanding oneself in the world as a whole person. There is much evidence of the growing interest in spirituality in the United States. In 1999, a Gallup poll showed that forty-eight percent of American respondents had talked about religious faith within the preceding twenty-four hours. Ninety-five percent believe in God or some universal spirit. Fifty-one percent said that they're too busy to enjoy God or to pray as they would like to. In a study conducted by Elizabeth Denton and Ian Mitroff titled *A Spiritual Audit of Corporate America*, the authors found that people do not want to fragment their lives; they do, however, see a strong differentiation between religion and spirituality. Spirituality does not mean religion, although for some, spirituality is expressed through their religious beliefs and practices. A

McKenzie & Company study found measurable benefits, such as increased productivity, reduced turnover and increased market share after engaging in training programs incorporating some elements of spirituality. There are a number of trends that have contributed to the increased need and interest in spirituality in the workplace. For example, Baby Boomers account for the largest generation on the planet, and they are currently at the age where it is natural to become more introspective of one's purpose in life. At the same time, we have Gen-Xers, who want something different out of their work life. They want more balance in their lives than their parents had. They also expect to bring their "whole selves" to work rather than separating their personal interests from their work. Another factor is the increasing diversity of the workforce, which has given rise to self-examination and a curiosity about different cultures and how differences fit together. Related to cultural diversity is a growing interest and influence of the Pacific Rim countries and the spiritual practices that Asians have been bringing with them to work for centuries. And speaking of global reach, advancements in technology have helped connect us in some ways and yet isolate us in others. Further, we now rely on technology to virtually connect us, but this has led to the longing for deeper personal connection. In addition, technology has contributed to the fast pace of change, which makes it almost impossible to stay in the moment or even to stop to reflect on values, meaning or relationships. Then there is the economic upheaval, which has made the contract between employee and employer temporary. Years ago, you would go to work right out of school or college, and you stayed with the same employer until you retired. Today, people look for security amidst uncertainty and are often forced to confront what to do next with their lives. Extraordinary stress and burnout exist in the workplace. As a result, absenteeism has been on the rise. In theory, companies talk about their employees as being their greatest asset. In reality, however, employees are expected to bring their work lives home and leave their home lives out of work. So technology, pressures from the economy, change, crisis, global influences and natural inquiries associated with age have contributed to an ever-increasing interest in spirituality at work.

Wright

In what ways can leaders incorporate their spirituality into their roles as leaders?

Cox

There are both internal and external aspects to incorporating a leader's spirituality into his or her role as a leader. From an internal perspective, a leader should spend time in self-reflection. First, we all need to understand our place in the world and our responsibility to those with whom we interact and lead. This means identifying core values, a sense of purpose and the qualities of attitude and behavior that align with those values and purpose. Once these characteristics have been identified, it is important that the leader continuously examine his or her thoughts and actions to determine whether he or she has been "being" in accordance or alignment with desired behaviors, attitudes and values. In addition, regularly making time to meditate, center or pray also helps to remove the bombarding stimuli and pressures of the external environment and allows the individual to connect with a clearer and higher consciousness. The external aspects of spirituality deal with how leaders express their way of being to the outside world. Interpersonal qualities such as truth, compassion, patience and humility are external expressions of the internal connection to spirituality. In addition, adopting the role of servant leader is a way of expressing one's spirituality. A servant leader is one who understands his or her responsibility to help create and foster a respectful culture that honors the needs and positive spirit of others and helps to develop each individual in the organization to his fullest potential. Further, this responsibility extends beyond the individuals inside the corporation out to the community, society and to the ecological environment. And finally, expressions of humor, creativity, art and nature are external ways in which a leader can maintain and encourage a connection to spiritual principles.

Wright

Can you cite any evidence that spirituality of the leader makes a difference in his leadership style or behavior?

Cox

One example I like to use is Michael Stephen, retired chairman of Aetna International, Inc. and the author of *Spirituality in Business*. Michael credits his spiritual practices for his success in expanding Aetna Canada's global reach into South America and Asia, resulting in unprecedented financial growth. He shares six lessons that he attributes to his success as a leader: patience, the power of silence, relationships versus tasks, the importance of meditation, the power of friendship and doing your best and relying

147

on the spirit of God for the result. Learning patience enabled him to be more in control, emotionally managed and able to reflect and appropriately respond. Silence, in this world of accelerated change, allowed him to observe, notice and be present with people. Making time for meditative practices allowed for centering himself and connecting with his own soul. Understanding that tasks are accomplished through relationships caused Michael to focus on building and fostering strong relationships. That led him to appreciate the power of friendship and the value of the people with whom he worked. The idea of doing his best and relying on the spirit of God for the results gave him the confidence in what he was doing and how he was doing it. Michael states that the leader has three roles: as a servant, to serve employees, shareholders and customers; as a shepherd, responsible for the well-being of the company; and as a steward, ensuring company goals are met through values-based and compassionate measures. His style and practices affected his ability to influence, motivate and impact the lives of those he led and those with whom he conducted business.

Wright

In your study of spirituality in the workplace, have you found any evidence that spirituality has any impact on the bottom line of companies?

Cox

Actually, yes. There are a number of ways of looking at that, and studies continue to be conducted. Ninety-five percent of Americans reject the idea that a corporation's only purpose is to make money. In addition, thirty-nine percent of the U.S. investors say that they always or frequently check on business' practices, values and ethics before investing. *Trend Report* of 1997 showed that three out of four consumers are likely to switch to brands associated with a good cause if price and quality are equal. *Harvard Business Review* showed that business owners credit eighty percent of their success to acting on their intuition. Intuition is only really found through quiet reflection. Further, the Domini 400 Social Index, which reflects the behavior of a portfolio of stocks that meet socially responsible criteria, has outperformed the S&P 500 since May of 1990 and continued to do so, even during the fall of the dot-coms. Customers, investors and employees will invest in or purchase stock based on some intrinsically spiritual principles.

Wright

How can a leader increase his or her spiritual quotient?

Cox

Spirituality involves self-awareness, meaning and connection. Therefore, leaders can increase their spiritual quotient by ensuring that they continuously focus on these three elements of their lives. Understanding as well as undertaking the responsibility of service, stewardship and shepherding will create a richer sense of meaning in the leader's life. Helping others find meaning in their work and giving others credit for what they contribute increases the effectiveness of the leader's spiritual quotient. This means engaging in acts of compassion, fostering effective communication and dialogue, having a sense of presence and holding up the highest intentions and values while being with others to help build connection and relationships. There are a variety of actions and practices one can engage in to increase one's S.Q., but much of it really boils down to asking the question, "Who am I being at this moment in time, and how will it affect myself and others?" And let's not forget to enjoy our work. We have seen this modeled in Southwest Airlines' philosophy of making sure everyone from the CEO to the baggage handler has fun at work so that work is meaningful and enjoyable.

Wright

I've been booking speakers for thirteen years, and a lot of times, when I talk about things like holism and spirituality, some of the meeting planners back off, because it's so hard to define. In all honesty, after having served on a church staff over the past forty years, when someone tells me she's not a very religious person but are a very spiritual person, I don't always understand what she's talking about.

Hendricks

I think the difference can be summed up by saying you can be a very spiritual person and yet be an agnostic, even an atheist, at the same time. Spirituality deals with understanding the connectedness that you have with other people and other things in the world and wanting to be a person of peace and integrity. Likewise, you can be a very religious person and not be very spiritual. For example, take some of the terrorists who base their war philosophy on religious beliefs. They certainly are not spiritual people. They may define themselves as people who are very religious, perhaps even religious leaders, but if they're preaching war and fostering hatred rather making peace and honoring others, I'm not sure that equates to being a spiritual person.

Wright

It would be hard for me to understand someone who made war and then said he was religious. I'm not saying it's not possible, but it would be difficult to understand it.

Hendricks

I think if we look at the 9-11 situation, we see religious fanatics who, based upon a particular interpretation of their religion, believed that they were operating in accord with their religious beliefs when they destroyed the World Trade Center and killed thousands of people.

Wright

Right. What can organizations do to elevate their entire leadership equation?

Cox

According to Richard Barrett, who's the author of *Liberating the Corporate Soul,* organizations build human capital by caring for the physical, emotional, mental and spiritual needs of their employees. They do this by establishing a culture of trust, meaning, community and ownership. According to a 1995 poll conducted by *Newsweek,* fifty-eight percent of Americans feel the need to experience spiritual growth. The quest for spiritual growth is expressed in connectivity and meaning. Work then becomes a place where people can actualize their sense of meaning. Organizations can help employees find personal fulfillment and meaning in their work by helping them recognize that through their work they are actually providing service—internally, externally and possibly to society. When employees are given interesting work, they have a sense of being valued and are encouraged to tap into their own creativity, skills and passions, which, in turn, enhances their productivity. When employees share the values of the corporation, and when people share and truly operate under a shared set of values and purpose, they create a sense of cooperation and community. Values, purpose and community foster a culture of belonging as well as a culture of trust. When trust is present, people are freer to take risks, to put their whole selves into the work, which, in turn, allows the community to leverage their skills, their perspectives, their experiences and their creativity. Communities operate with a particular dynamic of connection, belonging, commitment and strong relationships. In turn, there is a strong sense of desire to be of service to each other as well as generating a greater effort for collaboration. Finally, organizations that establish a culture of community and reward and recognition foster a sense of ownership through openness, inclusiveness and participation. This can only occur when leaders themselves are inclusive, open and encourage participative management at all levels of the organization. Most organizations understand the value of spirituality in the workplace. However, only about fifteen percent are really proactive in fostering spirituality. The truth is that many of them are afraid of it. A few, however, have led the way by implementing programs and specifying spirituality-related concepts in their mission statements. Merck and Medtronics, for example, have mission statements that incorporate high values. It's really about creating a culture of caring and having the employees recognize the culture as one that honors their spirit.

Hendricks

Just to put a bottom line on increasing the leadership equation, the bottom line is to hire smart, technically competent, emotionally mature, spiritually sensitive people. When you interview, look not just for intelligence but also for emotional soundness and the ability to care for others.

Wright

And if you can't, go ahead and develop them?

Hendricks

Absolutely.

Wright

We have been talking today to Deborah Cox and Edward Hendricks. They are founding partners of IgniteSpirit. IgniteSpirit is founded on the principle that identifying, honoring and encouraging each other's individual values, passions, talents, skills, essence and ways of thinking and learning will lead to an enriched, empowered and extraordinary working and learning environment. I want to thank you both for taking this time out of your day to talk to me. I really do think that you've made some progress in teaching me some things this afternoon.

Cox

That's terrific!

Hendricks

That's great! That's all we could hope for.

Wright

Thank you very much.

IgniteSpirit, LLC
16 Marigold Lane
Trumbull, CT 06611
Phone: 203.452.1557
Fax: 203.371.5103
Email, Ed Hendricks: Ed@ignitespirit.com
Email, Deborah Evans Cox: Deborah@ignitespirit.com
www.ignitespirit.com

Chapter 12

JOAN ELEANOR GUSTAFSON

Joan Eleanor Gustafson, an award-winning international speaker, is the author of three books on leadership and success. As president of Success and Leadership Dynamics, she works with corporations on leadership development and organizational productivity. She teaches graduation school programs on international management, marketing and e-business.

David E. Wright (Wright)

Today, we're talking to Joan Gustafson. She is the founder and president of Success and Leadership Dynamics. She is an internationally-known professional speaker, author and consultant. She has coached hundreds of individuals in achieving their desired results, both in their careers and in their personal lives. Prior to founding Success and Leadership Dynamics, Joan was a member of the Corporate Marketing Management Committee at 3M. During her twenty-six years at 3M, she had international leadership responsibilities in multiple functional areas, including e-business, customer satisfaction measurement, knowledge management, communication resources, sales and marketing productivity and information technology. In addition to her speaking and consulting practice, Joan is on the faculty of the University of Phoenix, where she teaches graduate level courses in international management and e-business. As a professional speaker, Joan has spoken to businesses and professional audiences throughout the United States, Europe, Canada and Asia. She is the author of three books on success and leadership. Joan Gustafson, welcome to *Taking Charge*!

Joan Gustafson (Gustafson)

I am happy to be here today.

Wright

Joan, in one of your keynote speeches, you stress the importance of developing leadership skills, especially intuitive and analytical skills. How does one develop intuition?

Gustafson

In my speech *Building the Leader Within You*, I talk about leaders using intuitive as well as analytical skills. I believe that we can all take advantage of our intuition, and we can fine-tune the intuitive skills we already have.

Earlier in my career, I was so busy with the things I needed to do each day that I didn't take the time to listen to the still, small voice within me. Then I attended a lecture where the speaker quoted Albert Einstein, who said, "Imagination is more important than knowledge." After hearing that quote, I started thinking about imagination and intuition and how they might play a role in my life. I found that my best ideas came to me when I was in the shower. This was the time of the day that was most quiet for me. It was the time that I listened to the random thoughts that entered my mind. When I started paying attention to them, my success as a leader increased significantly.

As far as developing intuition, I think we are born with intuition. Many of us just don't take it seriously. But I've found that when we listen to our intuition and, in some cases, combine it with analysis, we become more successful. Dr. Joyce Brothers said, "Trust your hunches. They're usually based on facts filed away just below the conscious level." That's what I call intuition.

Wright

Down through the years, several trainers have told me that intuition is a female skill, or at least women are born with more intuitive skills than men. Is that correct? And if so, can men develop intuition?

Gustafson

Although we have always talked about "women's intuition," it's not true that it is a skill only for women. Men also can be intuitive. Roy Rowen wrote a book titled *The Intuitive Manager*. In this book, he says, "Male or female, top brass or lowly trainee, the decision maker needs to understand how the brain constantly delves into the subconscious to retrieve buried fragments of knowledge and experience, which it then instantaneously fuses with new information." Leonard da Vinci said, "The ideas that would suddenly come to my awareness proved to be most worthy and were in the end found to be infallible in leading me to discoveries of great importance." Thomas Paine said, "Any person, who has made observations on the state of progress of the human mind cannot but have observed that there are two distinct classes of what are call Thoughts: those that we produce in ourselves by reflection and the act of thinking and those that bolt into the mind of their own accord. I have always made it a rule to treat these voluntary visitors with civility, taking care to examine, as well as I was able, if they were worth entertaining; and it is from them I have acquired almost all the knowledge that I have."

Wright

To simplify it, for me at least, intuition is an act of the subconscious mind being active and just coming to fore?

Gustafson

Yes. Intuition directly involves the subconscious mind in that thoughts or pictures just seem to bolt into our minds. When this happens, we usually don't even know the origin of these thoughts. They don't come from the analytical thought process that we're normally aware of using.

Wright

Leadership, it seems to me, is not only vision but also the ability to adapt in change. You've developed eight strategies, which help individuals accomplish their goals in the face of change. Can you briefly share them with our readers?

Gustafson

Sure. When I was going through one of the biggest changes of my life about eight years ago, I decided that I was not only going to survive the effects of these changes but I was also going to thrive and become an even stronger person because of the change. When I made this decision, I immediately wrote down eight action steps, which are strategies that can help people to survive and thrive during any type of change in life.

- **Number One:** Tune up your self-confidence. Think of yourself as the important person you are. Each of us is a miracle, and each of us has a mission in life and the skills, talents and abilities to fulfill that mission.

- **Number Two:** Take responsibility for stress reduction. There is a lot of stress accompanying any change, even change that we perceive as "good change." Three ways to reduce stress are relaxation, physical exercise and laughter. Bob Hope once said, "I've seen what a good laugh can do. It can transform tears into hope."

- **Number Three:** Focus on priorities. Ask yourself the following two questions: What are my priorities in life? Will this change affect me twenty years from now? This helps to put the change into perspective so that we can deal with it better.

- **Number Four:** Use your emotional energy wisely. If we spend time blaming, complaining, criticizing or condemning those who are responsible for the change, we're creating negative energy. This negative energy only drags us down, both emotionally and physically. Instead, if we concentrate on generating positive energy, we're able to deal with the change more effectively.

- **Number Five:** Look for the positive. Even though it may seem at first that the change has only a negative impact, we can find something positive if we look hard enough.

- **Number Six:** Maximize your productivity. During major change, people tend to spend time worrying about the future. However, worry breaks down productivity. When we're not productive, we again tend to generate negative energy. This becomes a downward spiral. Since worry does not solve any problems, I attempt to put the worry out of my mind. I encourage people to spend their time in looking at options and alternatives rather than in worrying.

- **Number Seven:** Create your own future. You have the power to create your future. In order to do that, you need to focus on your goals, priorities and alternative action plans for achieving your goal.

- **Number Eight:** Take time to enjoy your life. We are really on this earth to have joy. When I look at the word "recreation," I see within it the word "re-create." By taking the time to do the things that give us joy, we are re-creating ourselves, reinventing ourselves, refreshing ourselves and renewing ourselves.

Those are the eight action steps that I used myself when I was going through a major change. It helped me to really thrive on that change, and I have been teaching these action steps to other people since then.

Wright

Could you tell me a little more about using your emotional energy wisely? I didn't catch it the first time. How do you create that?

Gustafson

Any kind of emotion takes energy. Whether it's a happy, positive emotion or a sad, negative emotion, it takes energy. If we are using that energy in complaining about the changes or criticizing people who initiated the change, we are dragging ourselves down. We are using up some energy. If we can turn that around and look for the positive in whatever is happening, it can help to get us into an upward spiral during the change.

Wright

Almost everything in our culture is weighted negatively. We get a twenty-percent chance of rain instead of an eighty-percent chance of sunshine. When you get directions, someone will say, "Go down to the third stop light," but actually, it is a "go" light as well.

Gustafson

Those are great examples! It would help all of us to think about the "go" light whenever we are faced with a major change.

Wright

Almost everything—the war on poverty and almost everything—is stated negatively. It is really tough to be positive in this negative world. As a matter of fact, a man told me one day that at the sweep of any hour to turn to any radio or television station I want. He said he would give me ten dollars for everything positive that the announcer said if I'd give him a dollar for everything negative. I didn't want to take that bet.

Gustafson

No. You'd lose on that one, wouldn't you?

Wright

Talk to us a little bit about vision. What is your definition of "vision"? How can those of us who aspire to leadership develop the necessary characteristics?

Gustafson

The word "vision" derives from a word that literally means "to see." A vision is an image or a picture of the future. A vision is not just words; it's an actual picture. Leaders will start with this picture and then determine the steps for getting to this picture. In other words, they start with the end in mind.

Leaders collect the same data as other people, but they see more in this data. They show passion for their vision, and they inspire a shared vision by aligning people behind their vision.

Wright

Is the difference between leadership and management vision, or are there more characteristics?

Gustafson

There are definitely differences between management and leadership. When Dr. John Kotter from Harvard compared management and leadership, he listed the attributes/skills/responsibilities of a manager as well as those of a leader. For example, management includes planning and budgeting, whereas leadership is creating a vision and developing strategies. Management is organizing and staffing; leadership is aligning, motivating, inspiring and energizing people. Management is directing and controlling; leadership is establishing direction. Management produces short-term results—"short-term" being defined as one week, three months or six months. Leadership produces dramatic change. Leaders visualize results, not just for the near term but also for the long term.

Wright

While reading your book titled *Some Leaders are Born Women*, you quote a good friend of mine, Jill Lublin.

Gustafson

You know Jill?

Wright

Oh, yes. I've known her for many years. She used to do programs for me all the time. Jill says that, and I'm quoting her, "A leader is someone who is willing to take a stand, a person who is willing to get going regardless of how difficult things are at the moment or may be in the future." Taking a stand is more difficult in these days of decision by poll taking, don't you agree?

Gustafson

Definitely, it is. It's difficult at any time.

Wright

Also, isn't taking a stand a matter of character?

Gustafson

I think it is. We want people to like us. We want them to agree with us. When we take a stand, we are making ourselves vulnerable. They know exactly what we are thinking, what our goals are, what our thoughts are. There's a book that was written a long time ago called *I'm Okay, You're Okay*.

Wright

Right, by Dr. Harris.

Gustafson

Then there was another one called *Why Am I Afraid to Tell You Who I Am?* The answer was I'm afraid to tell you who I am because you might not like who I am. We want people to like us, so when we take a stand, we know that we might need to face rejection by some people. For this reason, it's definitely a matter of character. To take a stand, we need to have a strong belief. We have to be strong. We need to be ready to face adversity.

Wright

I remember how Dr. Harris's *I'm Okay, You're Okay* started the transactional analysis frenzy. There was another famous book afterward that added to it, which I thought was great psychology until it started turning people into volunteer psychologists.

Gustafson

I can appreciate that.

Wright

In your book, you devoted an entire chapter to it. The title of the chapter is Dare to Dream. It was interesting that you quoted several famous Americans' thoughts on dreaming. How does dreaming affect leadership?

Gustafson

When I talk about dreaming, I'm talking about intentional dreaming—not just daydreaming. I'm talking about visualization. Effective leaders have a vision, and they take time each day to visualize, or intentionally dream, about their vision.

May I take a few minutes to tell you how visualization works?

Wright

Sure.

Gustafson

This is a non-business example. When I attended the lecture where the speaker talked about intuition and imagination, he also talked about visualization. At first, I was very skeptical about visualization, but I was interested enough to give it a test, and I thought I'd give it a big test. I wrote down what my vision would be. My vision was that I was going to sell my house and build my dream home. At the time, my house had been on the market for eight months, and I hadn't had any offers. I had even reduced the price and still didn't have any offers. I had bought a lot for my dream home and had the plans drawn up, but I couldn't start building until I got the equity out of the house that I was living in. I decided my vision would be that I'd have an open house, and after the open house, I would receive a telephone call from my real estate agent. I visualized being at my house and hearing the phone ringing. In my vision, I walked to the phone, picked it up and heard the voice of the real estate agent. He would say, "Joan, a couple came to your house today, and they loved it. They made a full-price, cash offer, and they want to know if you can be ready to close and move out in two weeks." I thought to myself, "If I'm going to dream, I'm going to dream big!"

I closed my eyes and practiced this visualization exercise twice a day for two weeks. Then I had my open house. About two hours after the open house, my phone rang. On the other end of the line, the real estate agent said, "Joan, a couple came through your house today. They made an offer.

It's a full price offer, and it's cash. They want to know if you can be ready to close and move out in nine days."

I thought, "*Wow*! This visualization stuff is spooky." Then I thought, "No, it's a fluke. It probably would have happened anyway. It was just the time for it to happen." Finally, I decided to give visualization more of a test. I wrote down six more things I wanted to create in my life, and they ranged from career to relationships to financial things to material things to spirituality. All of my visions required a lot of stretch, like the first one. Within three months after starting to visualize, every one of my visions became a reality. I became a very strong believer in visualization.

Wright

I remember many years ago, success motivators took down Waco, Texas, did a lot of writing about visualization, and they made a believer out of me. Obviously, things happen in the mind, and it's just a small part of visualization. I remember I went to a workshop one time where a man had us close our eyes and visualize that we were cutting a lemon in two. We put the lemon in our mouth and started squeezing it. He started talking about the acid taste of the rind and all the lemon taste and everything, and I had to swallow so many times. I was salivating all over the place.

Gustafson

You could actually taste that?

Wright

I could taste it—everything that would have happened had I actually been eating the lemon was happening.

Gustafson

You were really engaged in the visualization, and your subconscious mind helped you to realize the effects of that vision.

Wright

Fortunately for me, my subconscious mind was really loaded, because I used to eat lemons whole with salt on them when I was a child—despite my mother's always telling me that it would eat the enamel off my teeth.

Can you give us some instances where women have excelled in leading others in their company to greater successes? I took a look at your book *Some Leaders Are Born Women*, and I was really fascinated by what everyone is talking about—the glass ceiling and all. You had some really great stories in there about women who excelled.

Gustafson

Yes. Some of the ones that I admire most are in that book and my other book, *A Woman Can Do That! 10 Strategies for Creating Success in Your Life* . One example is Lillian Vernon. You are probably familiar with Lillian Vernon catalogs. They've been around for a long time. She started her business at her kitchen table more than fifty years ago and has grown that business to over $259 million in annual sales. Her company employs 5,300 people during its peak season. It has eight catalog titles, two Web sites, fifteen outlet stores and a business-to-business division.

A lifelong philanthropist, Lillian Vernon has donated funds and merchandise to more than 5,000 non-profit organizations, including toys for the children of the victims of the World Trade Center and funds for the rescue workers. A role model for entrepreneurs and corporate executives as well as for millions of women in all roles and walks of life, she is one of the longest-serving CEOs in the United States. Her company was the first company founded by a woman to be traded on the American Stock Exchange, and more than twenty-three million Americans have shopped from Lillian Vernon catalogs.

Another is Ardath Rodale, a gracious woman who is chairman of the board and chief executive officer of Rodale, Inc. and chairman emeritus of the board of the Rodale Institute. She has authored three books: *Climbing Toward the Light*, *Gifts of the Spirit*, and *Reflections*. She has received two honorary Doctor of Humane Letters—one from Allentown College of Saint Francis de Sales in Allentown, Pennsylvania, and the other from Lehigh University in Bethlehem, Pennsylvania—and an honorary Doctor of Laws degree from Kutztown University. She is the mother of five and grandmother of ten. She is family centered and people centered.

She says her greatest aspiration as a female entrepreneur and leader of her company is to stand as a positive force for educating people everywhere in the process of helping the world build healthy soil to grow healthy food to feed healthier people.

She says their company purpose is to inspire and enable people to improve their lives and the world around them, and their values are:

- The Power to Heal
- The Responsibility to Listen

- The Passion to Innovate
- The Virtue of Teamwork
- The Value of Growth

People do not have to head up large companies to be considered leaders. An example is Vicki Tolman. Vicki's recent debut as an entrepreneur stemmed from family financial necessity. Deciding to become an independent sales consultant with Mary Kay, she vowed that she would be the best she could be at this profession. Within four months, she earned her first Mary Kay car, and she has earned many more awards since then. Although she has reaped some significant financial rewards during the short time she has been an entrepreneur, she looks at her business as more than the financial returns. She views it as a way to share the entrepreneurial spirit of caring and sharing with those with whom she works. Her energy, enthusiasm and genuine love for people are indeed contagious!

Wright

In your book, you also write about focusing on the power and the possibilities in people. Can you explain what you mean?

Gustafson

Effective leaders in today's world:

- Surround themselves with excellent people. Company leaders recognize that people are their greatest assets and get things done through other people.
- Generate excitement and enthusiasm.
- Create synergy.
- Align people behind the vision and strategies; inspire a shared vision.
- Develop cooperative relationships and partnerships.
- Expect the best from people and get it.
- Delegate authority along with responsibility.
- Contribute to the success of others.
- Recognize others for their contributions.
- Treat others with respect. Company leaders treat their employees as they would have the employees treat their customers.

Wright

You also advocate contributing to the success of others. Are you talking about mentoring?

Gustafson

Mentoring is one way to contribute to the success of others. I really believe that people who have been successful have an opportunity for continued success through mentoring other people. Other ways to contribute to the success of others are through recognition, encouragement, referrals and giving people credit for their accomplishments.

Wright

You would almost think that would go without saying, wouldn't you?

Gustafson

You'd think so, but it doesn't always happen. I've worked with some managers who take the credit for what their people have done. I always thought it was more important to give credit to the people who have done the work, because that inspires them to go even further, to do even more. This, in turn, contributes more to the organization.

Wright

Can your books be purchased anywhere?

Gustafson

They can be purchased from major bookstores, from Amazon.com and through my Web site.

Wright

Your Web site is?

Gustafson

It is www.leaderdynamics.com.

Wright

Joan, with our *Taking Charge* book, we're trying to encourage our readers to be better, to live better and be more fulfilled by listening to the examples of our guests. Is there anything or anyone in your life who has made a difference for you and helped you to become a better person?

Gustafson

Yes. There are several people who have really influenced me to become a better person. One is my mother, who set the example of care and benevolence. For the past fifty-eight years, she has been a full-time homemaker, wife and mother. Since her children are now grown, she spends an average of thirty hours a week doing volunteer work, making this world a better place for those who live in it. She believes in people and supports them in a positive way.

Another is my dad, who also set an example through hard work and perseverance. He has faced some difficult challenges, but he never gives up.

The third is my husband, who believes in me and constantly encourages me to reach new heights. He's my biggest fan!

I think I've grown through all of my acquaintances, especially those who have reported to me in a business environment. The people who have challenged me and some of my ideas are the ones who have contributed much to my success, because, through their challenges, I have learned to think deeper and to excel more.

Wright

Today we have been talking to Joan Gustafson, founder and president of Success and Leadership Dynamics. She is a professional speaker, an author of three books, a consultant and, as we have found out today, a great communicator. Thank you so much for being with us.

Gustafson

Thank you, and have a good day.

Joan Gustafson
PMB 296
3655 West Anthem Way, Suite A-109
Anthem, AZ 85086
Office Phone: 623.551.3881
Office Phone: 877.824.3014
Email: joan@leaderdynamics.com
www.leaderdynamics.com

Chapter 13

ALAN PARISSE

Alan Parisse is a seasoned executive with more than twenty years of front-line experience. As president of the Parisse Group, Inc., he helps organizations and their leaders deal with and benefit from technological, economic and social change. Billed as a "Street-Smart Intellectual" and "The Motivator for People Who Think," he is one of the nation's premier business speakers. His status has been confirmed by his having been named one of the "Top 21 Speakers for the 21st Century" by Successful Meeting magazine and by his election to the National Speakers Association's Hall of Fame.

David E. Wright (Wright)

Alan Parisse has the experience to guide organizations through their inevitable cycles of prosperity and challenge. With a combination of macro vision and key insight, Alan places organizational challenges and opportunities in their proper historical and philosophical contexts. He then helps develop the road map necessary for leadership and success in turbulent times. *Successful Meetings* magazine published a list naming Alan one of the "Top 21 Speakers for the 21st Century." So we are privileged today to be talking to Alan Parisse. Alan, thank you for being on our program, *Taking Charge.*

Alan Parisse (Parisse)

Thank you, David.

Wright

Alan, you've written that organizations must identify the successful attitudes, habits and beliefs that have worked for them in the past. Then they must determine if they are appropriate for meeting future challenges. Do success habits and beliefs change that much, really?

Parisse

Indeed they do, but not as fast or as often as we are sometimes led to believe. David, we just went through a decade where nearly everybody started believing in the "new economy." The mantra was that the world had fundamentally changed and that many things were immediately going to be very different. Economic cycles were history. Companies didn't have to worry about profits, and young people didn't need to get their degrees. Well, we now know most of that was nonsensical hype. So it may seem odd for me to say that some things really do change—but, of course, they do. The challenge is to avoid getting caught up in the popular beliefs of the moment and to determine when changes are likely to be both meaningful and lasting and when they are a passing fancy.

The first step toward meeting that challenge is to understand that most of us approach the issue of change with an inherent bias. We pretty much like the status quo, the lure of the familiar. That is especially true when we have been successful. When an organization or an individual has been a success, they become attached to the way they did it and the way the world was. After all, the way the old world supported them and the way they operated in that world worked. It's part of the reason many previously successful organizations have a particular problem dealing with significant change. When it comes to individuals, I have become convinced that the smarter we are, the more successful we have been, and the more thoroughly educated we are, the harder it can be to change. The old way was so good to us that we want to keep playing that game. The Navy's computer expert, the late Admiral Grace Hopper, put it very simply when she said the single most dangerous phrase in the English language is, "We always did it that way."

The next step in distinguishing meaningful change from the latest fad is to understand that there are different kinds of change. I tell my clients it is useful to break change down into at least three different categories: false, cyclical and fundamental.

The first kind of change is what I call false change. A lot of change that we hear about is not genuine; it is fake. It's motion that is presented as movement. Local television news shows often provide a wealth of examples. From day to day and week to week, they present very much the same news stories updating only a few facts. In fact, change a few facts and last month's news report is very much the same as tonight's. There is the car accident, a fire, a murder or two and some consumer outrage. Obviously, for the people directly involved there was a real change. For the community at large, however, these are mere anecdotes that illustrate long-standing trends in auto and fire safety, violence and business ethics. Nothing is fundamentally altered.

It certainly can be confusing, however. After all, the media do their best to keep things interesting. So they present what is, in fact, mere motion as though it is meaningful movement. Often, they try to extend an incident so it appears to be a trend. When there is a trend, it is often cast as destiny. Yet, much of what they talk about is really just false change.

The second kind of change is cyclical change, the ups and downs of business, investment and life. Cyclical change is certainly not new. Just ask a farmer. They know about cycles. In fact, we should all be experts in it.

Yet when movements are sudden and severe or when they last a long time, our emotions take over. When business or life is going down, many of us think it will keep going down until it dies. When the trend is going up, many of us start thinking it will go up forever. Of course, that's rarely what happens. Things go up, and things go down, and then they do it again. We all know it intuitively, but somehow we forget it.

The last category of change is a fundamental change. Every now and then, a deep-seated change occurs. Often, it is a technological discovery, such as the invention of things like moveable type in the fifteenth century, the telegraph in the nineteenth Century and, more recently, the Internet.

Sometimes the shift is political or sociological. History may well prove that what September 11 2001 created was a fundamental shift. Even more of a shift may well be the ability of terrorists to deliver weapons of mass destruction just about anywhere in the world. That is big stuff. It is real change.

Wright

So what do you say to these leaders in industry who say, "If it ain't broke, don't fix it?"

Parisse

Break it! Just on principle!

David, I am kidding—but only half kidding. The fact is that large organizations need both stability and innovation. The trick is to balance those conflicting demands. One way to do it is to innovate gradually in your base business while simultaneously forming teams of eager beavers and empowering them to try new things and new ways. You own it, but you don't control it closely. Let them break it for you.

One of the things that makes organizations inflexible is that they become slaves of their own measurements and labels. A good example was TQM. Back in the 1980s, U.S. companies wanted to catch up with Japanese quality. So we understandably started to define quality in measurable terms. After a while, we stop seeking quality and end up with our measurement of quality. Perhaps a better example that has been in the news lately is the never-ending need for ever-increasing quarterly earnings per share. As recent scandals have underscored, earnings-per-share has a way of becoming an end in itself. CEOs forget about building long-term value and contort the organization and its numbers to produce the earnings Wall Street wants.

On a personal level, an educator friend says one of the biggest issues troubled kids have to overcome is the way teachers and parents label them. Right in front of the child some say, "She's a little slow" or "He's not as smart as his sister." Many children get stuck with the label. She says that gifted children often have an even bigger problem. When they are treated specially, because they are gifted, they become very risk averse. They are very reluctant to take on anything at which they don't excel. But the same things happen to organizations. Once a hospital is named one of the best 100 in the land, they often worry more about retaining their status than achieving their true mission.

So leaders need to be careful how they define the game and how they label things.

Wright

I was interested in your statement about the military. You wrote, "The military history is largely a history of generals fighting the wrong war. They tend to use strategies and techniques designed for the previous war." With the problems that we're having right now with Iraq, do you think our military has taken this thought into consideration?

Parisse

I do. I'm certainly not a military expert, but it seems that one of the reasons we did so well in the Gulf War and again in the Iraq War is that we did not do so well in Vietnam. Understandably, generals are much more likely to fight the last war if they won it. The classic example was France preparing for World War II by creating an extraordinary line of elaborate defensive fortifications designed to protect its eastern border forever. The Germans easily outflanked the so-called Maginot Line by simply driving through Belgium and entering from the north. The line would have worked in World War I. The problem was that tanks, machine guns, artillery and aircraft had all become so much better that a linear defense was no longer effective. One of the first generals to see what later became so obvious was George Patton. He told his troops, "Dig your foxhole, you'll dig your grave." Patton was a controversial man, but he was fighting the war he was in. After Vietnam, our military seems to have learned its lessons well. In Vietnam, the military realized too late that fighting a traditional war against guerrilla tactics in jungles did not work. Before Vietnam, there were no Special Forces as we know and use them today.

Wright

As you speak and train America's corporations, how do you suggest they develop new ways of seeing, thinking and acting in the future to ensure their success?

Parisse

I start by pointing out that management is really a new skill. In the mid-nineteenth century, a large business had a hundred employees. Even government wasn't big. Abraham Lincoln's staff consisted of his cabinet and two and then three secretaries. Just a few years later, we had U.S. Steel, Standard Oil and a growing government. Back in the mid-nineteenth century, few people had any idea how to manage large organizations. That's why the military and the church became the model. Hence, the hierarchical organization chart was born, with the boss at the top and the layers of minions below.

Historically, the leader at the top got power from such things as:
* position, title and trappings
* the ability to hire, fire and assign work
* control of information and access

- physical capacity and force

These days, all of those sources have lost much of their punch. *Dress for Success* was a best selling book in the 1980s, but a quick walk around many an executive suite today would show that things have changed. With many tech execs sitting in cubicles and Warren Buffet living in Omaha, there is a much lower correlation between trappings and power. Similarly, the ability to hire and fire doesn't have the juice it did before. That was especially true a few years ago, when there was such a shortage of employees, but it's still hard to find good people. Losing a job isn't the catastrophe it once was. My dad called himself a "salary slave." He stayed with one company for forty-four years. Why? He was a child of the Great Depression. If he lost that job, we were in trouble. My mom didn't work until much later in life, and there weren't many good jobs for woman. On top of that, there wasn't that much of a social safety net. So managing my dad was easy. He would put up with almost anything.

Not only have memories of the Depression faded, many families today have two incomes, and there is a much more substantial social safety net. As a result, today's leaders don't get nearly the same power from their ability to hire and fire. In fact, Peter Drucker suggests that today's workers are closer to volunteers than the "salary slaves" of fifty years ago. That calls for a different leadership style.

Controlling information and access to information was once a major source of power. Information funneled up to the boss, and he or she doled it out. Now, anybody with an access code can get most all the information the CEO gets.

It wasn't that long ago that employees were subordinated in part because the boss could do every job in the house better than anybody in the house—or at least thought he or she could. And it also wasn't that long ago that the foreman at the Ford plant took the guy out back and beat him if he was giving him trouble. Physical capacity was part of what made the boss the boss. Now, doing every job better is almost impossible, and "getting physical" results in a lawsuit. So we've had a real shift in how leaders have to go about influencing their teams.

Wright

You work a lot in the area of leadership. I've heard that the difference between management and leadership is vision. Do you believe that to be true?

Parisse

It's an important difference. Managers play the game. Leaders define the game. Doing that well takes vision. Managers solve problems. Effective leaders create problems—positive problems—and that is an art. A manager must maintain stability and order. A leader's job is to create some chaos—controllable chaos. Positive chaos.

More than having a vision, however, a leader must communicate that vision—live it. As Albert Schweitzer said, "Example is leadership." On top of that, a leader must sell his or her vision. When General Eisenhower became president, Harry Truman, his predecessor, confided to friends that Ike would have a problem, because generals are accustomed to ordering people around. The president has to sell the Congress, the people and sometimes his own cabinet.

Wright

Do you ask your corporate clients to establish mission statements and communicate their visions to their employees? If so, could you give our readers an example of how they might start the process?

Parisse

One of the things that I feel very strongly about is that leaders must focus themselves and their organizations—in other words, pick their shots. While these are often general platitudes, properly done, a mission statement can help a leader focus the organization.

In the 1980s, I was elected president of a large trade organization for a one-year term. While traveling to the first meeting, I sat next to my mentor. He had been president ten years earlier. He asked to see my goals for the year, and I proudly showed him my list of thirty-eight. He laughed and said, "Alan, pick one." I was stunned. I had waited a long time for this and had my list. He said, "You don't understand; the year's already over. If you go for thirty-eight things, all you will do is get a lot of things started but nothing will be completed. Pick the one thing or maybe two things you won't give up on."

Leaders who want to make a positive impact on their organizations must understand that they will not be remembered for thirty-eight things but only for one or two. The key is to pick it, to choose what you want to be remembered for. You were the one who—what? Cut costs? The one who helped us survive through a difficult time? Increased revenue? Restored quality? Put the customer first? Leaders should pick their one and let the entire organization know it is their mission. No compromise here. Everything else is negotiable. So when I talk about mission statements, I talk about the fact that the leader has to get in his or her one. What do you stand for? And that's a big part of your mission statement.

Wright

Alan, many times, things go wrong in America's companies. Failures are often reported. In your opinion, what is the single biggest mistake that leaders or managers make that is the costliest to them.

Parisse

Two come to mind. The first is failing to create a context within which the leader gets fast and accurate feedback. It's a rare leader who is getting the truth from the people around him or her. Of course, that is especially true of autocratic leaders. Saddam Hussein probably wasn't getting very good feedback. To a lesser degree, feedback is a problem for most all leaders. Most subordinates are biased toward laughing at the boss's jokes and saying what the boss wants to hear. One solution is for leaders to encourage intellectual insubordination from their team. If that doesn't work, they have to demand it.

The other mistake is related to the first. It is allowing their organization to be dominated by one or more of their functions. Henry Ford was a manufacturing genius, but his organization suffered from imbalance. Not only did he utter the infamous remark about giving customers any color car they wanted so long as it was black, he ignored other functions. At the start of World War II, Ford didn't have an organizational chart or even a reliable balance sheet. Their banks told them how much money they had. To cure the problem, they brought in Tex Thornton and his Whiz Kids.[1] They were numbers people who got the financial side straightened out. But they forgot about the cars, and the quality of the cars fell off a cliff.

Other companies overemphasize sales or deal making or even quarterly earning per share. Now there is nothing inherently wrong with any of those things. We are talking about getting out of balance. While there is great value in having all employees understand and support the need for the other functions to perform, it is dangerous when critical functions are ignored or confused. Bottom line: The CEO who makes salespeople focus too

---

[1] The Whiz Kids by John A. Berne 1993

much on accounting issues will see sales fall. The CEO who makes his accountant a salesperson may be headed for jail.

Most leaders give lip service to balance, but when there is a crisis, they rely on a few advisors with a narrow focus—one similar to their own.

Wright

You write that technology has been transforming manufacturing, finance and distribution for decades. So it's now time to reinvent selling. Could you explain what you are talking about?

Parisse

Just a few years ago, the mere suggestion that salespeople had to change the way they sold brought the response that people are still people and sales doesn't change. While there is a kernel of truth to that, the fact is that technology has had an enormous impact on the sales process. One of the biggest changes, of course, is the Internet, which has created alternative distribution methods that do not require a salesperson. In the old days, it could be said that nearly all sales objections boiled down to one core objection: Can I trust you? This was especially true in intangible sales such as life insurance, securities, et cetera, where the objections included: Can I trust your ability? Can I trust your integrity? Can I trust your concern for me? Those are still important questions, but now there is another entire line of questioning that did not exist a decade or two ago: Do I need you? Can I point and click around you? That is a very significant shift.

Nowadays, both tangible and intangible salespeople must continuously illustrate to their customers and their management that they add value. To do that, they have to be part of the process. They have to do more than just make contacts and make sales. In industrial sales, they have to be scouts. They have to be talking to customers and bringing information back to the company to make sure that their product lines are up to date and that the company knows what their customers are thinking, feeling and doing. They have to be involved in the process, and, literally, the salesperson becomes part of the value. For example, when an organization buys a new computer system, they are not just buying a computer system, a mere commodity. They are buying professional advice and service. So salespeople must be more.

Years ago, I met a fellow who was ahead of his time. He was a top IBM computer salesman in their heyday. Over lunch, I said, "Come on. Your products are good, but they are not the best, and they are certainly not the cheapest. How do you sell so much?" At first, he responded by talking about their software and service. When I pressed him further, he said, "When push comes to shove, I tell them they're getting me. They're not buying a computer; they're buying me—twenty-four hours a day, seven days a week. I give them my home number." He was part of the value. Technology is now such that salespeople must add value beyond just the sale.

Wright

I was impressed with an article you wrote on personal success. Along with other suggestions, you advise people to focus on others, stay positive and don't give up on their goals. Could you talk about that for a minute?

Parisse

When times get tough, there is a temptation to give up on goals. Clearly, when difficulties appear, it makes sense to review one's goals and priorities. Adjustments are often appropriate. That said, however, one should be careful not to merely give up on his or her goals. Usually, it makes a lot more sense to retain important goals and merely extend the timeline. People need goals to stay motivated, and so do organizations.

This is one more area where leaders can help or hurt a lot. When there is a fire burning, it has a way of getting attention. In most cases, leaders should keep at least one eye on the longer term to help their people set positive goals and stay motivated.

After all, apathy can be a considerable problem. You know, David, it has been said that the opposite of love is not hate; it is apathy. When times are good, people do feel and act like youngsters in love. When times get tough, at first a few become angry. After a while, however, the dominate emotion is apathy. It is my sense that the apathy comes in part from a lack of positive goals.

In the short run, mere survival may be the only goal, but after a while, survival becomes exhausting and apathy arises. When layoffs loom, goals usually go out the window as people become so worried about their jobs, they stop doing them. After the reductions in force, a lot of people are saying something like this: "We used to have seven people in our department, and we worked hard getting our jobs done. Now we are down to just the two of us. We work all these hours, and we can't do our jobs. All we do all day long is put out fires."

Let's be realistic. If the world or their company really has changed so fundamentally that those old goals are folly, then they have to be let go. But most downturns are cyclical. In such cases, leaders should help their people understand the situation, eliminate goals that are no longer attainable and then realistically extend the time line on the rest. "I was going to do this in two years; now I'm going to do it in five." In many cases, what we find is the opposite. Leaders begin to manage the fires and either lose sight of company goals or continue to push for goals that don't fit the current cycle.

One other thing people can be doing in difficult times is looking for the silver linings. It is usually true that at least some opportunity lies hidden in difficulty. Some kernel of good, or potentially good, news is buried in bad. Finding it keeps people from getting discouraged. It keeps them on a positive track.

Wright

What a great conversation. I learned a lot today, and I appreciate you being with us, Alan.

Parisse

It's my pleasure. Thank you.

Wright

We have been talking today to Alan Parisse, who has been guiding organizations through cycles of prosperity and challenge for a long time. Now we know why *Successful Meetings* magazine named him one of the "Top 21 Speakers for the 21st Century." Alan, thank you so much for being with us.

Parisse

Thank you.

Alan Parisse
1630 30th Street, PMB 310
Boulder, CO 80301
Phone: 303.444.8080
Fax: 801.382.6308
Email: alan@parisse.com
www.parisse.com

Chapter 14

JIM TUNNEY

A celebrated and respected speaker, Jim Tunney's credentials place him in the top one percent of professional speakers working today. A past president of the National Speakers Association, he continues to serve on its Foundation Board of Governors and is a mentor to many members. Known for his ability to educate, motivate and entertain, Tunney works with national and international corporations and organizations, helping them to build winning teams, develop leadership skills and increase personal productivity.

David E. Wright (Wright)

Jim Tunney had an exemplary career as an NFL referee from 1960 through 1991. The first official to be named to the All-Madden team, Jim also won top honors from the National Association of Sports Officials, the Gold Whistle Award in 1992 and is in the National Football League Hall of Fame. In his thirty-one years as an NFL official, he received a record twenty-nine post-season assignments, including ten championships and three Super Bowls. Jim, thank you for being with us on today on *Taking Charge.*

Jim Tunney (Tunney)

David, it's my pleasure. I'm glad to help and hope I can be of value to you.

Wright

Jim, in your book *Impartial Judgment,* you write, and I'm quoting you here, "As an official, I don't care who wins. Officials want only to see the game played fairly, not necessarily evenly, because some teams are better than others, but fairly, within the rules." As you speak to America's companies and given the events of the past few years having to do with dishonesty, do you believe the same could be true of the American corporations?

Tunney

No question about it, David. First of all, regarding the book *Impartial Judgment*, I wanted to title it *Because I Don't Care Who Wins*, but the publisher thought that was a little long for the title of a book. The publisher is the one who came up with the idea of *Impartial Judgment,* that the official is impartial in his judgment. He's just calling the fouls as the rules dictate him to call them. One of the things that I've been most proud of since 1960, when I started with the National Football League, is the high degree of integrity of its officials. We have never had an official accused of, or maybe even approached, about bribery or throwing a game or anything like that. When I look at the personality of an official, I first look at his level of integrity. Does he operate his life the same way he operates the game on the field? When I speak to corporations and businesses, I always include a segment on integrity. I believe that in the business world the number one key in being successful, retaining your business year in and year out, is the sense that you're just going to be honest with people. I quote my dad often, because my dad was very influential in my life. My dad said that what he would like his four children to be when they grew up was to just be good. Just be good people. If you're a good person, that's what comes through. If you're a good person as a manager of a business or a salesperson, whatever job you have, being good is what it's all about. Doing the right thing. Not just doing things right, but doing the right thing. And you know, we all have a sense of the right thing. We all know what is right. And I just can't believe that we go back into Wall Street and see some of the things that happened there a few years ago. We've recently seen the Enron scandal and things like that. What in the world were those people thinking? We could never operate a football game with that kind of mentality. When you operate a football game, the people in the stands, the 70,000, want to know if this guy is fair. Is he honest? Is he going to do the job? They want to win the game, but they want to be sure the guy in the field does things fairly. That's the thing that I like about officiating, the thing that I tried to emphasize to the crews that I was fortunate enough to work with over the thirty-one years: What's the right thing to do?

Wright

It really surprises me, as you said, but it really surprises me that these corporate heads were taking four- and five-million-dollar salaries and their stockholders were losing money. Now that was really strange.

Tunney

Not only in that area but also there is a woman in jail today because just recently, we're talking since 2003, she has been indicted for stealing 1.9 million dollars from the United Way.

Wright

Goodness gracious.

Tunney

Here's a charity to which we all give money to help people in need, and I don't know what her title was, but she stole 1.9 million dollars from them, and they indicted her, and she's in jail now. What was she thinking? How in the world do people get this kind of mentality? What do they think they're getting away with? Has greed taken over? I know in the game of football, the coaches, the players, the fans, they want to win, and they'll do anything they can within the rules to win. Sometimes a player or a coach may go beyond the rules but not very often, and they don't do it with any intention to cheat; they do it just because they want to take every advantage they can. But is that the right thing to do? I have a good friend whom I'm writing another book on right now, Herman Edwards, who is the head coach of the New York Jets. He says, "Just do the right thing." He is such a strong advocate of a high level of integrity that his story needs to be told. I think that's the way the game of football ought to be operated, by doing the right thing.

Wright

When you wrote about being a referee, you said, and I'm going to quote you again, "The thrill that comes from witnessing excellence is part of why this work never gets boring." Could that not be said about any leadership or management position when viewing teamwork on the job or at work?

Tunney

Let me quote the people at the New York Jets again. Herman Edwards became the head coach in 2001 and said that everyone, from the caretaker to the security guard to the owner, "Woody" Johnson, said, "It's a pleasure to come to work with a head coach like Herman Edwards." What he does, in doing the right thing, is be very positive about things. He's honest with things. If you've made a mistake, he sits down with you and tells you where you went wrong, what you needed to have done and how he feels it needs to be corrected. He's about helping people do a better job. I think that's really the opportunity that I see on the football field. As I saw Bart Starr or Johnny Unitas or Joe Montana or John Elway as a quarterback come into the huddle, they knew that they were going to get the job done. Everybody in the huddle knew that they were going to get the job done. They were there to help the team do a better job. Now that's what leadership ought to be. A manager in any organization ought to be helping with teamwork by being somebody who, first of all, has the abilities to do it and, second, helps other people raise their levels of ability so that they can do the job the best way.

Wright

Johnny Unitas was one of my heroes growing up. Since I'm from the University of Tennessee, I'm glad that Peyton Manning won the Johnny Unitas award.

Tunney

He looks like Johnny Unitas. He has the same high-top shoes, but he also has the same kind of a forward neck as John. As I watched Peyton Manning operate, and I've known his dad Archie for a long, long time, he runs a football team like Johnny Unitas did.

Wright

That's great. Having led companies for many years, I'm a little bit impressed with the insight that you have about winning. You write that "A shared goal always comes before a shared victory." How do you teach leaders and managers in corporations this lesson?

Tunney

I use the statement that organizational behavior is reflective. Top to bottom, inside and out, organizational behavior is reflective. That means that the guy at the top is sharing his goal or her goal, how this company ought to be going toward victory. And it's not a secret of what we should be doing. It's something that I share with people and reinforce with the people whom I work with all the time. I share our goal. I share our procedures. I share our mission. I share everything that'll help this company be better. Before we can ever get to a victory, which ought to be shared as a team victory, it ought to be a shared goal before it can be a shared victory. So you've got to communicate to people what you want them to do. You've got to be clear. I often use this definition of communication: Communication is not just the message that you send but the response you get. If you're not getting the response that you want, then your communication has fallen short. Be sure you communicate over and over and over to your people what you want to happen.

Wright

Jim, you have written that as an NFL official, you were rated more on the mistakes you've made than on the number of correct decisions, which I think is unfortunate. But you go on to say, "We get a better idea of how to do it right if we know clearly what is to be done. In that sense, it is irrelevant to know what we've been doing wrong." How do you convince America's teachers and coaches of that truth?

Tunney

That's an interesting way to put it. The way I put it, we were graded on the number of mistakes we made rather than the number of good things we did. I never did like that kind of system. It's what we call downgrading rather than upgrading. You downgrade people, because the managers at that time, the supervisors officiating, were seeing who had the fewest mistakes. I don't think that's the way to run a corporation. I've argued that with the National Football League for a long time. You don't run a corporation based on the fewest number of mistakes. Rather, you should run an organization on the greatest good that they do for the organization. What we do learn—and we've known this for years in all kinds of sports—we learn from the mistakes that we make. You take the time to look at the mistakes and say, "Okay. Here's the mistake, and here is the way we need to correct it." We need to take the mistake we made and see how we can improve on it. What happens in a team situation, and I think it happens in businesses also, is when something goes wrong, you analyze it more carefully than when it went right. For example, if a team wins a game, you say, "Gee. We won the game." You spend less time looking for the ways to improve yourself. If you lost, you'd spend more time looking for ways to improve yourself. That's the essence of that statement. The essence is you look for better ways to do it when a mistake has been made. But I don't think you can run an organization successfully for a number of years and have people become successful in that organization by looking at just the mistakes. You need to compliment them on their victories. Ken Blanchard, the one-minute manager, has an organization called Blanchard Training and Development with a staff of 300-plus people. I said, "Ken, what is your job there?" He said, "My job is a cheerleader. I go around and help people do a better job, and you do that by complimenting people." I've always believed that you build teams by building people. You don't build teams by tearing people down. You build teams by building people. So when they make a mistake—okay, they make a mistake. It's constructive criticism. How do we get better at this? How do we make this a better effort next time?

Wright

You talk a lot about visualization in performance. Could you explain to me and to our readers what visualization is and give us a few tips on how to do it?

Tunney

Visualization is a vital part of any success. It is so important in the world of sports. We can see it in the world of sports more than we can in business. If you look at Tiger Woods, for example, he has great skills as a golfer, but what we don't see in Tiger is his ability to visualize where he wants to hit the ball. We see in Michael Jordan his great shooting ability, but we don't see that inside his head, he sees the ball going in the hoop. You should never, as a basketball player, think of anything other than the ball going in the hoop. As a golfer, you should never think about anything rather than where you want to hit the ball. I learned that as I was teaching driver training in the city of Los Angeles. We would drive down the main thoroughfare, and here was this fifteen- or sixteen-year-old student behind the wheel. I was on the right side of the car, and all I had was a brake; I didn't have a wheel. As the car would sort of drift toward the side of the road, I would say, "Don't hit that car, don't hit that car, don't hit that car." Well, what I was doing was saying, "Don't hit that car." The student wasn't seeing the word "don't," she was seeing the words "hit that car." It's important to say the positive rather than that. So I learned to say, "Keep your left wheel near the white line, left wheel near the white line, left wheel near the white line." Reinforce that visual so that you say what you want to happen rather than try to say something that you shouldn't. I also hear people say, "Don't forget your purse," "Don't forget your bag," "Don't forget your suitcase,"

"Don't forget this." What are you saying? "Don't forget." Say it the other way: "Remember to pick up this," "Remember to pick up that," "Remember, remember, remember" rather than "don't forget." The mind seems to eliminate the word "don't." It's important we visualize what we want to happen. To give you one more example, I was talking to Dick Fosbury, the fellow who invented the "Fosbury Flop" in high jumping, where he goes over the bar backwards. I asked him, "What do you do when you're getting ready to jump?" He said, "I'm visualizing myself going over the bar, every step of the way, jumping over the bar. I can see myself doing it." I asked, "Well, when you visualize yourself, Dick, don't you sometimes see yourself knocking the bar off with your elbow?" He said, "No. Why would you picture failure?" With visualization, we don't want to picture failure or we'll fail. Picture success so we'll move toward success. Our mind dictates what our body is going to do, so we picture success. We mentioned Johnny Unitas or John Elway or Joe Montana as a passer. They pictured throwing the ball where the receiver was going to be. They saw that picture in their mind before they threw the ball, and they threw it to that point. They didn't throw it to where the receiver was; they threw it to where he was going to be. They pictured visualization in a positive way.

Wright

Jim, you write that your dad, who is also a coach, didn't buy into the idea of stars. He appreciated commitment and excellence. What impact did your father have in your life, and were there others who helped shape the values that you hold today?

Tunney

I was very fortunate to have a father who set the kind of values, as I mentioned to you before, like being good, just doing the right thing for people. He coached a lot of great athletes in his day as a coach in high school and was associated with a lot of athletes over the years. The name Tunney was important to our family, because at the time my father was growing up, Gene Tunney was the heavyweight boxing champion of the world. There is no relationship family-wise that we can identify. Dad admired the fact that he was a world champion, but, as the old expression goes—he put his pants on one leg at a time, like everybody else does. He recognized the value of a commitment to excellence, but that person wasn't any better than anybody else. That person just did the best thing that he could. My dad helped me understand the values of excellence and that you want to strive for excellence. If you work for excellence, you'll soon achieve it. Lombardi said, "You must always seek perfection while perfection may not always be possible. If you seek perfection, you'll capture excellence along the way."

Wright

That's a great quote.

Tunney

That's what it's all about—trying to be the best that you can be. If you talk to any person in any walk of life and ask, "Would you like to be better than you are?" they'll say yes. "Would you like to achieve excellence?" Yes. It's always positive that way. Then they say, "But I don't think I can." That self-doubt is the thing that really knocks you down. My dad helped me overcome any self-doubt, and I had some as a kid. I doubted whether I could be any kind of an athlete. I wanted to play in the major leagues—I didn't have that talent—but he never one time said, "You don't have enough talent to be in the league." He said, "Just keep working at it and let your own abilities dictate where you can be." That kind of value helped me. When I started in the National Football League, I was thirty years of age. I was on the field with some players who were older than I was. They were the best in the National Football League, and I thought, "Do I have a right to be here? Do I deserve to be here?" My dad taught me that I could hit the pitching. He used that expression a lot: "You can hit the pitching." He said, "The mound is still sixty feet, six inches, whether you're playing in the minor leagues or the major league. The difference from the minors to the majors is the ball comes at you a lot faster. If you believe you can hit the pitching in the minor leagues, then you can hit the pitching in the major leagues. You're there because you deserve to be there." Those kinds of values reinforced the fact that I had a right to be in the National Football League. I just had to rise to that level of excellence, because I was dealing with players who were the best at what they could do.

Wright

Sometimes humor can go a long way toward reducing stress and allowing people to relax in order to do their best. You write a humorous story about the great Paul Hornung at the first Super Bowl. Could you repeat it for our readers?

Tunney

Paul Hornung was a Heismann Trophy winner out of Notre Dame. When the Green Bay Packers drafted him, he was there before Coach Lombardi got there. When Lombardi got there, he had heard of Paul Hornung's sort of wild reputation off the field. He loved partying. He loved going out. Paul loved being with people. Paul still is that way; he loves being with people. Vince Lombardi made Paul Hornung a better football player, because he took the abilities that Paul had and worked them into his system and kept Paul in line, in a sense. Vince Lombardi was a very strong disciplinarian, and in my book *Impartial Judgment*, I dedicated a whole chapter to Vince Lombardi, comparing him to my father. I called it Strong Understandings, because my dad and Lombardi seemed to have the same sort of values. His values and Paul Hornung's values were not the same.

When they went to the first Super Bowl on January 15, 1967 in Los Angeles, the NFL played the AFL. There were rival leagues for a number of years before they finally got to play what they call the World Championship Game; they didn't call it the Super Bowl. So there was a lot of pressure on the National Football League and on Vince Lombardi to be sure that they were the dominant leagues. They were in the coliseum in Los Angeles before the game, working out. As they walked up the tunnel to the locker room, Paul turned to Coach Lombardi and said, "Coach, could I say a few words to the team before we go back out for the game?" Lombardi was really worried about that, because he never knew where Paul was coming from or what he was going to do. Paul being the wild kind of a guy that he was, and given his off-field antics and the nightclubbing and everything, Lombardi was very concerned. Finally, he thought about it and said, "Okay, Paul. You can." So just before they went on the field, Lombardi said, "Paul would like to say a couple of words." Paul got up and said, "Gentlemen, I came to Los Angeles for two reasons. I conquered one of them last night; let's go out and get the other one done today." The whole team sat there and laughed. It took the pressure off. It took the tension off, and they went out and beat the Kansas City Chiefs 35-10.

Wright

I remember that Hornung won the Heismann trophy in 1957 and took it away from John Majors from the University of Tennessee.

Tunney

That's right.

Wright

In your book, you talk about some of the coaches, such as Lombardi and Halas. You speak of them almost reverently. Were these men of great character? What was it that drew you to them as role models?

Tunney

When I first met George Halas in 1960, it was almost like meeting Thomas Edison. This guy had invented the game. This is a guy who created a thing called professional football in 1920, maybe even 1919. He decided we could play professional football, and we could pay the players to do it. Halas would go around after the game and pay the players in cash. Some would have a great game, and he might give them $25. If you had a very good game, maybe you'd get $100. Those were the kind of times, and that was the kind of money they dealt with in those days. He would have a whole wad of cash and would deliver the cash after the game. He had a sense that in the National Football League, it was not about the players; it was about the team. It was about creating an organization where people worked together better. Halas was very strong in team efforts. Lombardi picked up on that team—and I have a picture on my wall that I'm looking at right now—of Lombardi in an overcoat and Halas in a Chicago Bears jacket, standing in Wrigley Field, talking before a game. It's a classic picture of two gentlemen who really understood the value of professional football. It was not so much a business for them. It was also a four-letter word called G-A-M-E. It was a game that they felt they could play and be successful with and bring people together, bring the best together—the best possible players they could get—and create a team effort. I like the values that they transferred to their team in the team effort and teamwork concept.

Wright

You designate an entire chapter in your book to People Make the Game. Could you give us some examples, and is the same thing true in business?

Tunney

I've said for years that I think Lombardi could have been the president of Texaco or U.S. Steel or any organization, because he had a sense of bringing people together. But besides the people in the game, besides Lombardi, I've seen great people like Tom Landry, who had a sense of integrity that was second to none. Tom would never do anything dishonest on the field. I see people like Don Shula or Bill Walsh or Chuck Noll or people who just have a sense about bringing people together and making them feel part of the team, of helping them achieve something that maybe they never thought they could achieve. Don Shula, the winningest coach in football—who had more winning victories than George Halas—also has the record for the team that went seventeen games undefeated in 1972. That's an important accomplishment, but he did it through a sense of believing in himself and helping an organization believe in itself. This is why I refer to the coach of the New York Jets, Herman Edwards. He has a sense of people believing in themselves. On the cover of his play book, he has a statement that says, "It's the will, not the skill." What he says is that everybody in the National Football League is a good player. They're all skillful players. But it's the will, not the skill that takes you to excellence.

Wright

As a professional speaker, you pride yourself on the opportunity to teach self-reliance and personal accountability. You write that your aim is always the same—clearer motivation and peak personal performance. Tell us what you believe motivation is and how we can become better motivators.

Tunney

First of all, motivation comes from within. You've got to have the will to do it yourself. Other people can help you. Other people can give you ideas. Other people can show you the way. The way you show people, I believe, as a coach or the head of an organization or the coach of a football team, is to do it by example. You walk your talk. You do what you ask people to do. If you want them to be motivated to do a better job, then you've got to be motivated to do a better job. You've got to demonstrate by your actions, on or off the field, that you are indeed trying to do the best job you can every single day. When you come to work, it's a good day. It's a good opportunity for you to be better at what you're doing. You should look at every day as an opportunity to ask, "How can I do better at what I do? How can I do more for myself? How can I do more for other people?" Take the team concept, a simple example of eleven guys on a football team or fifty-two players on a squad, and translate that to your community. What can you do better for other people? I've used the statement an awful lot of times, "I can't do all the world needs, but the world needs all I can do." That's the kind of motivation that helps people become better at what they do.

Wright

Jim, since you addressed the subject in your book, could you tell us your opinion of instant replay? Also, is there a sense in which leaders and managers can use instant replay in their companies to ensure better learning and more success?

Tunney

Absolutely. Let's take the instant replay in the National Football League first. When it first came in 1986, the supervisor officials called me to a meeting before the season and said, "We're thinking about putting in this replay. What do you think?" I said, "Do I get to vote?" They said, "No. You don't get to vote. That's up to the twenty-eight owners." I said, "What are you asking me for? Because if you want to put in the instant replay, I'll work within your system. If you want to make the field 120 yards long instead of 100 yards long, that's okay. If you want to make the ball more round like a soccer ball instead of a football, that's okay. You decide the rules; I'll work within those rules. So if you put in instant replay, I'll be able to work within those rules. That'll be fine." Some of our officials in the NFL said at the time that putting in this replay would intimidate them. That they would have a playoff on Sunday afternoon, make a decision and then the replay would reverse it, and they would end up being wrong. Then they would have to go to work the next day and somebody would say, "Boy, you sure made a mistake there. You sure screwed up." How would they deal with that? I took a different position. I said to our crew of seven—as you know there are seven officials in the NFL crew— "Let's see if we can operate with what we call in business 'zero defects.'" I said, "For example, if Buick makes a thousand cars, and 999 of them are good cars, and you buy the one that isn't very good—we call it a lemon—you buy the lemon. Buick, in your mind, is a bum. So if we do everything we can as well as we can but we still make mistakes, they're going to think of the mistakes, not the good things we do. So let's talk about zero defects. Let's see if we can go through the entire season in 1986 without making any mistakes at all." So our crew worked 156 plays for fifteen games with only one mistake—one for the entire season. One reversal from the instant replay. We had other mistakes, but not necessarily from the instant replay. We had one instant replay mistake. When we did that, I said, "That's great. One. But it's not zero. Let's see if we can do better." So I took the position that instant replay can make us better officials. I think that's what we should do in management. We should talk to people about how they can become better at what they do. If they make a mistake, it's okay, it's all right. Everybody is going to make mistakes. I've made them, too. I've had to admit to coaches that I've made a mistake. I remember making a mistake one time in a game with Philadelphia and Dallas. I blew the whistle too soon. The coach was furious with me. I just walked over to him and I said, "Coach, I blew the whistle too soon. I made a mistake. I'm sorry. There's nothing I can do about it. My fault, but we're going to have to play it right here." He told me later on, "There is nothing you could've said to me that would have disarmed me more than saying that you made a mistake." He said, "I've made mistakes, my players have made mistakes, people make mistakes; it's okay. You were honest enough to admit that you made a mistake, so let's go on from there." As managers and leaders of people, what we can really do is help people to understand that when we do make a mistake, let's see if we can learn from that mistake and be better people because of it."

Wright

What a great conversation, and I want you to know how much I appreciate you taking the time out of your day to talk to me today.

Tunney

It is my pleasure, David. My pleasure.

Wright

Jim Tunney has been known as the Dean of NFL Referees ever since Bob Oates, Jr. of the *Los Angeles Times* tagged him with that back in 1978. As we have found today, he's taking those same principles that he learned in all of those years of working with such excellence into America's corporations to teach and train leaders, managers and employees. Thank you so much for being with us on *Taking Charge.*

Jim Tunney Associates
P.O. Box 1500
Carmel, CA 93921
Phone: 831.649.3200
Fax: 831.649.3210
Email: Jim@jimtunney.com
www.jimtunney.com

Chapter 15

PHIL HOLBERTON

Since 1996, Phil Holberton has been an adjunct professor at Brandeis University and has enjoyed a thriving practice of business advisory services that focuses on senior-level coaching to organizations, specifically in leadership development. He works with individuals and organizations to develop goals and accelerate their achievement. In 2001, he began publishing Speaking of Leadership®, *a biweekly electronic e-zine specializing in business and leadership strategies.*

David E. Wright (Wright)
Today, we are talking to Phil Holberton, an executive coach who works with executives facing specific problems or demanding challenges. His presence brings an objective perspective to top-level management and an ability to offer suggestions based on years of authentic life experiences. Relying on a solid foundation of business experience, Phil helps other executives identify and achieve results, use sound business practices and maximize their natural talents so they may grow. He, of course, is a proven leader and also teaches leadership at several universities. Phil helps individuals and companies grow. Phil, welcome to *Taking Charge*.

Phil Holberton (Holberton)
Thank you, David. I'm pleased to be here.

Wright

Phil, you've said that leadership is a lifelong journey. Can you explain that concept?

Holberton

My students ask me all the time, "Phil, are leaders born, or are they developed?" My response to them is, "Leaders are like athletes. Some have more natural talent than others, but if you practice your leadership skills day in and day out the way Michael Jordan practiced basketball when he was a youth, you will grow to be a very effective leader."

It's that simple. Leadership really is something we have to practice day in and day out, and we can't take it for granted. As businesspeople, we need our leadership skills to become as second nature to us as our thinking about market share, pricing or other business issues. We need to think about how we're treating people and whether we are generating willing followers for our leadership. Good leadership is one of those disciplines we can learn all our lives.

Wright

How has your own leadership style changed over time?

Holberton

When I first got started in business, I was one of those people who thought they had all the answers. I was pretty well educated, and I came in with a very strong point of view and would try to micromanage people. I quickly learned that didn't work out very well!

One of the things that I've learned over the years of my leadership development—as a result of being an executive—is that to truly become a leader, a person must transcend from having all the answers to seeking the answers. When you're looking out into the future, the future is full of uncertainty. We don't know all the answers; we may know how to do certain things in a particular environment, but certainly we don't know all the answers to the inordinate number of possibilities that lie ahead for our organizations and for us. For that reason, a wise leader doesn't try to come to the table with all the answers. He or she doesn't say, "This is the way you should do it, and you have to do it this way, because I know better." Because more likely than not, the leader's top-down solution will be wrong. Instead, the wise leader's job is to help the group find the right answer, to solve the problem together with his or her team, whether that team is the organization or a department. That's an important lesson I've learned over my career. Now I no longer believe I know all the answers. Every day, I realize how little I know and how much I have to learn. It's particularly common for young leaders to believe that they have all the answers. They are often brimming with a confidence that almost borders on arrogance. But I'm a great believer in the concept of "servant leadership," which boils down to the belief that we as leaders are here to help others grow. If we make that belief our attitude, if we get outside of ourselves and really put the other person, the team or the organization at the forefront, we grow as leaders. And we're also much more *effective* as leaders. A great leader is one who can get his or her followers excited and passionate about the vision the leader is trying to achieve. Nobody in this world wants to be told what to do; but if we can, with our followers, develop an environment that excites them—a vision that they really want to follow—then we've really matured and grown not only as successful leaders but also as significant leaders. Significant leaders are leaders who help other people achieve their goals and also give back to society.

Wright

What leadership skills did you have in the very beginning of your career? Which one of them did you believe needed improvement?

Holberton

When I was first getting started in my career, I didn't really have much understanding of leadership. And I didn't really think much about leadership, either. Of course, I had grown up in a family environment that taught me good values. I think I've always operated from a philosophy of "doing unto others as you would like to have done unto you" and of treating people with respect. Using that as a core foundation, I was able to quickly recover from any mistakes that I made when working with individuals.

The most important leadership attribute that I had to learn was to sit back and listen more. Now I always tell my students and the people I work with that God gave us two ears and one mouth and that we should use them in that proportion. Unfortunately, early in my career, I was probably using my mouth twice as much as I was using my ears—and I think that got me into trouble. So I learned! I didn't change my values; my values have always been solid. But learning to listen helped me improve my leadership skills over time. A lot of leadership development is on-the-job training. You try things, and you figure out what works and what doesn't. In my case, my on-the-job leadership development was highly augmented by two leadership seminars I attended after I had been in business about ten or fifteen years. One of the leadership seminars was put on by the Center for Creative Leadership in Greensboro, North Carolina, and the Levinson Institute in Boston offered the other. Both gave me a frame of reference for what leadership is all about. In particular, the Center for Creative Leadership offers a week-long program that includes laboratories, simulations, games and lots of testing. When I took my first 360-degree diagnostic assessment of my leadership skills at the Center, I was pleasantly surprised by some of the findings. But I was a little unpleasantly surprised to learn from the assessment about how I had come across to some of my peers. It was a tremendous opportunity for me to get some important insights from a professional leadership education program. I could—and did—then go back and use those insights in my place of employment to become a more skilled leader. Now I spend a lot of time teaching and talking about peer relationships, helping others to learn from the lessons that I've gained over the years.

Frankly, early in my career, I thought managing and leading were one and the same thing. I thought that if you were a manager, you were automatically a leader. What I've come to learn over time is that managing and leading are distinctly different concepts.

Wright

Someone told me the other day that the difference between leadership and management was vision.

Holberton

Vision is, indeed, one very important element of leadership. Leaders need to look forward while managers are trying to work in the day-to-day tactical setting. For example, a leader's job is to make sure that his or her team is being effective and is working on the right endeavor. Then the manager's job is to make sure those endeavors are being worked on accurately. Managers are not necessarily making choices about what to work on, but they want to make sure they and their staffs are very efficient. Leaders, on the other hand, need to make choices about *what* to work on. That's the primary difference.

Wright

Who were significant role models in your life, from a leadership perspective? And what role did mentors play in your leadership development?

Holberton

I didn't even know what the concept of mentoring was when I started in my career. When I joined a company right out of college, my first boss took me under his wing. He was a mentor to me, and I learned a tremendous amount from him, both personally and professionally. My first boss not only was a mentor but he also was a significant role model for me. By example, he really taught me how to mentor others. Although he didn't have to, he mentored me and nurtured me along. When I wasn't, perhaps, feeling quite up to a task, he would give me the encouragement I needed. And that's another role of a leader; when people feel they are stuck, a good, effective leader is going to give them the support they need and, if it's necessary under certain circumstances, perhaps a push. If I am your mentor and I support what you do, even if you make a mistake, we'll learn from our mistakes. A good mentor will help you deal with the issue of making mistakes and help you learn from them. Today, I not only lecture and talk about mentoring but I write about it as well. I believe seeking out mentors is one of the most important activities any young developing leader can undertake. Seek out those who have been there before you and learn from them. Again, its part of seeking answers rather than thinking you know all the answers. If you are willing to be open and seek someone who can add perspective, coach you and help you understand what your leadership future might look like, you can shorten your learning curve and really blossom and grow as a potential leader.

Ever since my experience with my first boss, I've always tried to seek out mentors along the way. Even though I do a lot of mentoring myself now, I still seek people who are far ahead in some aspect and who can add value to my life now.

Wright

Were there any watershed events that helped propel you to the next level in terms of leadership development?

Holberton

Interestingly, a prime watershed event for me was that at one point in time I lost a job, unexpectedly, during an economic downturn that eliminated my position. I then began to network to look for a new position. Ironically, that experience of constant interaction and networking with other individuals did more to develop and help my career than almost anything! For one thing, it taught me that work just isn't about me or about the organization that I'm working with—that it takes a network, a community, to really enable one's life to be fully effective.

And now, to this day, I teach and I lecture about networking and what an important skill it is for effective leaders. There has been some work done by other academics that suggests that those managers or aspiring leaders in organizations who network within their organization—by that, I mean developing relationships with people in other functional areas—are going to be more successful in their careers than those who don't. Tom Peters has referred to this as "management by walking around," but it's more than that. It is about really developing relationships with people. If you do that, when you need to solve problems, you can go to those individuals and work with them, because you've already developed the relationship; people then will respond much more effectively. The watershed event in my career was being thrown into a situation where I needed to network because I had to find a job. But I then took that skill of networking and learned how to use it effectively in every other position that I've been involved with. Since that time, anything that I've achieved in my professional career has come as a result of having been networked into a situation where I had already developed a relationship. People want to do business with people they like and respect. Networking is a way to develop that friendship and that relationship.

Wright

You describe networking as an important attribute of leadership. Can you explain it to us?

Holberton

Networking is one of those business skills driven by opportunity and business conditions. You see it used more and more: Businesses form alliances and partnerships with other organizations, even those that are sometimes competitors. To successfully operate in today's fluid business environment, I believe you need to be open to collaborating with others. The best way to collaborate is to seek relationships with others where there is implicit trust. That takes time to accomplish.

When I talk about networking as a leader, I don't mean just collecting business cards and putting them in your Rolodex. I'm talking about developing relationships with people. As you build sincere, friendly relationships with people over time, you are able to call them, compare notes, make suggestions, propose ideas and so forth. Those relationships can help you achieve a level of success that you otherwise never could envision. Being an active networker can really help you shine.

As you can imagine, some people don't feel very comfortable networking. I teach leadership to software engineers, and some of them are individuals who like to stick to themselves and focus on their own specific activities. I keep encouraging my students to take risks, to reach out and develop good networking relationships. They will feel better as human beings, and ultimately, they will find that networking helps their careers and helps them progress.

Wright

Are there other areas that we haven't covered that are important to your leadership development?

Holberton

I'd say one of the traits that you need in order to be a truly effective leader is not to be one-dimensional, not to be focused totally on your job. I think you need to have balance in your life. Areas that need to be in balance include not just your professional work but also your physical health, your mental health, your emotional and spiritual health, your family and your finances. I'd say that, early in my career, I didn't have all the aspects of my life in balance. I was so focused on the business side of my life that I let some of the other aspects slip. I've learned over the years that if you're truly going to be on top of your game—if you're really going to be an effective leader—you need to have all the areas of your life in balance. Recently, I interviewed a noted entrepreneur in the Boston area, Desh Deshpande, who has founded several companies. Desh puts it this way: In life, we juggle several balls—work, family, friends and your own philosophy. These balls are crystal balls, except for the work ball, which is a rubber ball. If ever you get into crunch time and have to drop a ball, make sure to drop the work, because the rubber ball bounces back. If you ever shatter the other balls, it is very difficult to get them back.

I think Deshpande's story is a wonderful metaphor for how important it is to try to keep our entire life in balance in order to be effective not only in our business environment but at home as well.

Wright

It is a great metaphor. I've never even heard or thought about that before. What a great way to explain it to us. You talked about your personal life. What role did your personal life play in your development as a business leader?

Holberton

Unfortunately, because I was so focused on my business world, I dropped one of the breakable balls early in my career and ended up divorced. I then went on to have a second family. I'm blessed now with a thirty-one-year-old married son, a twenty-nine-year-old married daughter and a twelve-year-old son. I've learned now that keeping my whole life in balance is very important in helping me be an effective father and a leader. I can be a lot more effective now that I can keep my life in balance. I did learn from the experience of dropping one of those crystal balls early in my career, and it hasn't happened again.

Wright

I know exactly what you're talking about. When you consider the decisions you've made through your life in business, in leadership, in other areas of your life, for that matter, has faith played an important role in your decision-making process?

Holberton

There's no question that faith is an important component of my life. When I was out of a job and had to look for one, I was positive that faith and spirituality were going to lead me to a good result, that I was going to end up finding a job that was attractive to me and that I was attractive to. During that job-hunting process, my faith grew enormously, getting stronger and stronger each day. Since then, because of my deepening faith, I've become a senior leader in our church. At one point in time during my tenure as a senior leader, when our church was going through a change in clergy, I felt I was almost half clergy, half layperson, because I became totally absorbed into the day-to-day activities of the church. To this day, I do pastoral calling on my fellow parishioners who are sick or in a time of need.

I believe that part of leadership is reaching out and helping other individuals. When you are in a frame of mind where you have "emptied your cup" of all your anxiety and you are in the present—centered and in the moment, helping another human being—that's when you are going to be most effective as a leader. That is part of keeping your life in balance through faith and spirituality. I don't mean religion per se, but I think spirituality and peace of mind are really important components in gaining total fulfillment in life.

Wright

Absolutely. Returning to your theme that leadership development is a lifelong journey, can you speak to that from your own experience?

Holberton

Every day I continue to learn from those around me. I'm a big believer in opening up the possibilities and learning from others. I don't ever want a day to come when I feel like I know all the answers and don't continue to grow. The fun part of being a leader and the fun part of participating in life is that you are learning all along the way.

Wright

What an interesting conversation. I really did learn a lot today, Phil. I appreciate the time you took today to do this interview.

Today, we have been talking to Phil Holberton. He works with executives facing specific problems or demanding challenges. He is an executive coach and he helps other executives identify and achieve results, utilize sound business practices and maximize their natural talents so they might grow. He, of course, is a proven leader as we've just found today. Phil, I really do appreciate you talking to us today.

Holberton

David, thank you very much, I really enjoyed participating in your interview.

Phil Holberton
151 Tower Rd; Lincoln, MA 01773
Business: 781.259.9719
Mobile: 781.259.9724
Email: pholberton@holberton.com
www.holberton.com

Chapter 16

SHIRLEY K. TROUT

Calling herself "The Laughter-Learning Link," Shirley helps adults laugh while they're learning and helps kids learn while they're laughing. Shirley is president of the Association for Applied and Therapeutic Humor, is a member of the National Speakers Association and is a professional speaker and corporate trainer. She will receive her Ph.D. in Leadership Studies from the University of Nebraska in 2004. She is author of Light Dances: Illuminating Families with Laughter and Love, Humor in Your Home Doesn't Mean Your Home is a Joke! *and numerous classroom and training curricula on topics from parenting to banking.*

David E. Wright (Wright)

Today, we are talking to Shirley Trout. Shirley is a diverse professional communicator who calls herself, "The Laughter-Learning Link," because she helps adults laugh while they are learning and helps kids learn while they are laughing. Shirley is a veteran professional speaker and member of the National Speakers Association. For nearly thirty years, she has been a professional writer and editor and is a talented photographer. She is currently completing her Ph.D. in Leadership Studies from the University of Nebraska. Seen as a leader in diverse venues throughout her entrepreneurial life, Shirley is currently using her two-year presidency of the Association for Applied and Therapeutic Humor to redesign the leadership structure to allow the association to become more inclusive and to allow for growth, both nationally and internationally. Shirley is employed as a training development specialist with a national financial services consulting firm but is perhaps best known for having a hand in the success of her training and traveling companion, "Izzit A. Live?!" Ms. Trout, welcome to *Taking Charge*.

Shirley Trout (Trout)

Thank you, David. It's nice to be here today.

Wright

Can you give us a little idea of how you got into the field of leadership?

Trout

Looking back on your life, I sort of figure that it actually started long before I ever, ever thought. I was involved in leadership just by virtue of having parents who threw me out in front of people, saying, "Go do something, and be proud of it once it's over." But I discovered that I really started to lead individuals and groups when my children were in elementary school and I was a young mom just in my twenties. People kept asking me to do things, and I just kept saying yes. Even though I didn't necessarily have the skills at the moment, for some reason, I apparently thought that I could learn the skills I'd need.

I was kind of a stay-at-home mom—although I didn't stay at home very much, because everybody was always asking me to do things—but when you're a person who is *available* and when you're a *willing* person who is available, you soon find plenty of opportunities to serve as a leader. I wasn't tied down to a traditional employment schedule. In a small community, they need for you to volunteer your time, and, like I said, I kept saying yes, and I kept learning more things, and people kept asking me to do more things, and I kept saying yes. Over the course of time, then, you sort of start realizing it's actually setting you up for some leadership roles in a very short time.

Wright

In what ways has your formal education and your real-life education impacted your understanding of leadership?

Trout

I actually have had a lot more real-life experiences than formal training, although I am in this Ph.D. program now and just loving it. A number of years ago, at one of the NSA events, I heard Ian Percy, who's a philosopher from Canada, talk about how to be successful based on two scales: the "how" scale and the "why" scale. I will never forget his message. You just need to hear those things when you're right at the moment where you *need* to hear them. And all of a sudden, they sink in like he's talking exactly to you.

Anyway, in Dr. Percy's message, he said, "If you get your 'why' right, your 'how' will come naturally." That's true, *except* that sometimes you need to know *what* you need to be working on. It's not just the how and the why. So my *why* was right, and my *how* could adapt. I could figure that out, but I didn't know for sure *what* needed to be done in a number of areas.

When I got into my formal education and started studying leadership and then reflected back on my life—where I had actually served as a leader a number of times to that point already—all of a sudden, I realized there are really *three* scales. The leadership studies—the formal education like Kouzes's and Posner's work with the Leadership Practices Inventory and Bass & Avolio with their Transformational and Full-Range Leadership— actually tell us *what* needs to be done to be an effective leader.

Kouzes and Posner identified the five practices of challenging the process, inspiring a vision, enabling others to act, modeling the way and encouraging the heart. Boy, are those ever true! When you start looking at leadership in action, those things are so on target. Of course, there's Bass & Avolio's work with Transformational Leadership and the four "I"s that they discuss: Idealized influence, Inspirational motivation, Intellectual stimulation and Individualized consideration. It's really been exciting to get into leadership first and then get to study it and then really get to see just how profound the work in leadership research is in an applied way.

Wright

I felt that same way about psychology. When I was taking psychology courses as a young person just beginning school at the university, it was all theory. Then I started operating companies and, at one point, had about 175 people working for me. And with all of those interactions, I went back to the university to study psychology again. All of a sudden, I said, "Oh, *that's* what they meant."

Trout

Exactly. The research just brings the applied so much to life. I'm sure there's a lot of research that goes on that is not nearly as applicable as it's been in my experience. But boy, some of these researchers have really helped me understand. I was leading intuitively to some extent, but now that I'm in significant leadership roles, I'm really using tested techniques of leaders deliberately. That doesn't mean that I'm doing everything *right,* but I sure have some clear guidelines to help guide me.

Wright

When did you first think of yourself as a leader, and how has that impacted what you are doing today?

Trout

You have to understand, I come from a small town in Nebraska, and we farm for a living. Most of my experiences have emerged from my involvement in this small-town environment. The first time I ever thought of myself as a leader was at a church finance board meeting. I had served on that committee for a few years, and then I was off for a while and then got back on. When I got back on, I was so disgruntled, because these people were talking about the *same things* that we had talked about *six years before,* when I had been on the board the first time. *Nothing had been solved*!

All of a sudden, I just started asking questions like, "What were we going to do about it?" At first everybody kind of looked at me like, "What are you talking about, 'doing something about it'?" Apparently, we were just here to kind of hammer it around, you know, but not actually *solve* any problems. Anyway, I decided at that moment that I needed to kind of push people to actually follow through. *Somebody* needed to make something different happen so we weren't having these same discussions six years later! That was actually the first moment that I recognized that, yes, in fact I can make a difference, and if I apply my skills, I will. That was the first time that I recognized that people *want* someone to step up and help them make some decisions and provide some direction.

Wright

Can you tell us a little bit more about your companion, Izzit A. Live?!

Trout

Yeah, Izzit?! is actually this funny little phenomenon in life. I attended a humor conference a number of years ago, and in the trade show, I plucked Izzit?! out of the masses of critters in this one booth that was selling puppets. This little chimpanzee puppet since then has become my lifelong companion. And people—even if they don't remember me or my name or my message—they remember my monkey. Anyway, it's just a character, but when he's on and with me, he is so lifelike that he just causes people to stop in their tracks. They get to do a real interesting little kind of a dance in their brain. It's like, "This can't be real, but it *is* real!" So I have a lot of fun with him, and like I said, people kind of know me as "The Monkey Lady."

Wright

I'm glad it's something tangible. I was afraid that we might have to carry you off.

Trout

[Laughing] No. As a matter of fact I kind of carry *him* around.

Wright

Besides Izzit?!, what leaders have you looked up to or learned from who have influenced you in the way you lead today?

Trout

You know, I look back at the historical leaders; Abraham Lincoln is huge with me, Winston Churchill, Gandhi and actually Machiavelli. It's been real interesting in these leadership studies. There's been a girl who has gone into Machiavelli's writings and really looked at what he was actually teaching. He has been misrepresented, at least the way she has analyzed it. In fact, he was able to change his leadership style to accomplish what he wanted, but what he was wanting was really very beneficial to his people at that time. So even though a lot of times people will say you're Machiavellian if they're meaning you will do *anything* to get what you want, if you look at what his life really stood for, it was actually *adapting* your leadership style to get people to continue to follow you toward the good of the group. She explains that this quality is very consistent with practices like the Individualized consideration in Transformational Leadership. It's just a little different twist, and I'm kind of intrigued by that.

Then the other mentor I had was my father, who was really involved at different levels in community and state government. He just inspired me with the way he demonstrated his fairness and levelheadedness, and he was very focused with what he wanted people to do. I mean, he really wanted people to get involved together and break down all kinds of political barriers and that kind of thing. He was also an amazing leader for our family, and he not only led us with direction and expectations but he helped us *laugh*. My sisters, brother, cousins—*everybody* in our family knew we were going to laugh a lot when he was around. It was *great!*

Then, going back to those others, I like the juxtaposition of Gandhi and Churchill. Churchill was such a phenomenal man, but he was so committed to a certain outcome. Gandhi has this soft passive resistance thing. His life was all about working with people in almost an invisible way. It's a servant leadership style that causes people to really stop and think about their values. So those are some people to whom I look up.

Wright

What has being president of a national association taught you about leadership?

Trout

It kind of goes back to what I've discovered about how much value the academic studies bring to the applied world. I realize that some people really just chide academic work, because they say it just isn't worth anything in the applied world. But that has not been my experience at all. I have really asked the board that I have at the Association for Applied Therapeutic Humor to accept trusting me to take them into a radically different structure and way of operating so we can get more done. We're getting more people involved. Not everybody is from the old guard. I brought in new people, and it's been very, very interesting.

I have been watching how the leadership practices identified by Kouzes and Posner and with the Full-Range Leadership principles apply in reality. I'm watching how the individuals react to the challenges of this change process. I'm keeping those very specific things in my mind as I'm working with this group as they are accepting how to see themselves differently and what that means. I've challenged them, and they are inspired, but I've also helped them see a new way of getting some systems and policies in place so they can actually get things accomplished. If I've not heard from an individual—and we have eighteen on our board right now—I'll make certain that they hear my voice on the phone, asking how things are going and checking up to see if they need anything more from me or anyone else.

So what this experience has taught me about leadership is that it's critically important that you lead with some knowledge and with very specific purpose. Recognize that you can really change the course of the future for your organization or whatever level you are leading if you truly understand the principles and follow them. But you have to continue to monitor how far to push and when. For example, I've already realized that there's a radical change that we need to make—*beyond* where we are right now. But I can't ask that of them yet; it's too soon. They're already learning to adapt to one radical change, and we have to let them plateau and get comfortable with this initial change before I or my successor can take them to that next level.

The other thing I've learned is that I have to *keep studying*! You find out, when you're in a position where people are counting on you—needing you— that you have a lot yet to learn, and there are no excuses. You just have to learn what you don't know and study hard to fill that gap. You have to be prepared with good information when people need you.

Wright

I was told many years ago in a leadership conference by a man that I really respected—we were talking about leadership, and he was discussing the fact that leaders are not born— "Leaders are leaders only because the people who are the followers respect him enough to call them leaders." As a bottom line, he said, "David, if you think you are a leader and you look around and no one is following you, you're only out for a walk."

Trout

Right!

Wright

I've never forgotten that. Do you think he pretty well hit the nail on the head?

Trout

Oh, absolutely! I mean there *is* no leader if there are not followers. A kind of fun way to look at leadership is to look at followership. Like he said, you soon realize that you have to have good followers in order to be a good leader. There's no small art in that, either! I had an experience with that in leading this group into change. There was a point at which the "old guard"—they were not old in age but were some of the founders of the organization—were starting to stir up a little undercurrent of discontent. But one of those people chose to get me involved. We do a lot of things on e-mail, so she chose to get me involved in the discussion and allowed me to dispel the myths that were starting to grow. In doing that, she demonstrated to me a *tremendous* leadership of her own because she trusted me. She was a wonderful follower at that moment. You know, if she had not made the decision to let me address some of those comments, even though they were inaccurate, they were kind of taking off, and those misunderstandings and skeptical attitudes were going to take on a life of their own. But as a fol-

209

lower, she brought me into it and allowed me to get involved so I could intervene before any damage was done. As a leader, I truly appreciated the way this person served her role as follower!

Wright

I see that you have written a couple of books on parenting and some that focused on parenting with humor. How do parenting and leadership and humor and leadership fit together?

Trout

To me, they're all one and the same. Parenting is one of the greatest opportunities to lead that any person will ever be given. As a parent, you actually help mold an individual's behavior and mindset. That's leadership! And you can't do that without humor. Humor is a wonderful thing, because it gives you a perspective. It uses a different way of looking at things to end up letting you see a joke or to chuckle at yourself for something that happened or chuckle at another person for the way it happened. Leadership involves seeing a situation from many perspectives and then being able to set a course or a direction based on those perspectives—based on that vision you have of how those perspectives can come together.

You know, there were high-level peace talks going on between the U.S. and the Soviet Union a number of years ago, and it was getting real tense. And so the facilitator stopped the discussion and said, "We need to stop and let everybody tell their favorite joke." There was this dead silence for a little bit. Finally, a Russian leader stood up and said, "What is the difference between Communism and Capitalism?" He said, "In Capitalism, man exploits man. In Communism, it's the other way around." It just totally broke the tension of the moment. And the story goes that the talks proceeded smoothly following that humor intervention.

Humor makes it so the group can continue to move forward. So even though it may seem a bit obscure, I think parenting is one of the purest forms of leadership, and humor is the social lubricant that helps you implement the skills necessary to lead—including leading a family.

Wright

I've got a forty-one-year-old daughter, a forty-year-old son and a fourteen-year-old daughter, and they—

Trout

[laughing]

Wright

Every time I say it, everyone laughs! See, I don't see the humor.

Trout

You don't see the humor?! I'm laughing because I had my surprise just eighteen months after my third kid was born. And I remember at the time telling the doctor, "I don't mind having surprises, but I am *so* glad it's coming now instead of twenty years from now."

Wright

That's the truth.

Trout

So congratulations! Fourteen, huh? You're going to need my book *Light Dances: Illuminating Families with Laughter and Love*! I have to say that slowly or people think I'm saying *"eliminating* families with laughter and love!"

Wright

I *am* going to need it. My daughter goes into high school this year. I get to live through that again.

Trout

Oh, my!

Wright

I also know that you have a corporate job developing training materials.

Trout

Yes. Don't you just love the way my life just tracks so cleanly—one thing and then another—all so logical?

Wright

Oh, yeah!

Trout

You can just see exactly what I'm all about, can't you? Since I started saying yes to things years ago, it has never stopped. You know, these bizarre things come along, and I just keep saying yes. Usually I need the money! You know, I'm getting to the point where, I'm just eager to try something new. But they just asked me, so I thought, "Heck, I haven't tried corporate America yet. Why not?" Of course, the humor is one of the things,

211

because it's like, "Well, here's another one of life's jokes. Let's try corporate now!"

But you know the whole concept of leadership is just so profound in every single environment where I've gotten to spend some of my life. It really is an amazing phenomenon. People sometimes scoff at me: "How can you *study* leadership?" Well, live life! Start looking at leadership and see what it does!

Wright

Is developing training materials for this financial services consulting firm a growing interest of yours?

Trout

Actually, training is something I've been involved with through the years, so it's not necessarily a *growing* area of interest. It was just something I could say yes to and actually know how to do it, for once! But the fun thing that's really come from it is that this is the first time I've gotten to "play" inside the corporate world. And I've gotten to see leadership from inside that kind of environment. It's so important in every environment! I've been in education and non-profit and in community-based experiences and now in corporate. And it's just these constants, these leaders, are in every single environment. The leadership makes all the difference in the world. And to find a *good* leader is such a treat! Good leadership truly is an art.

Wright

There is certainly a lot of diverse entrepreneurial life. I hate to use that word, "entrepreneurial," because it applies to me. How is this entrepreneurial background impacting you today?

Trout

It's like I said—having gotten the opportunity to see leadership in action from a variety of perspectives and seeing that leadership simply makes that huge difference in every single aspect of life, whether you're talking about the family or the church or the corporation or the non-profit. I was involved with a non-profit for a few years that had *dreadful* leadership. And I just got a call not too long ago from the secretary at the time, asking if I wanted to take any of the things from the office, because the organization was folding. You know, that *is* the future of some organizations if they have the bad fortune of having leaders who really don't know how to lead.

Wright

It's a shame, isn't it?

Trout

It is. I mean, the work that that organization had set out to do was so profound, but the leadership literally took it to its knees. And then you get involved with an organization that is just about to fall, and you bring a good leader in, and in a very short time, they're building buildings and making money—securing funds!

Wright

That happens in churches a lot.

Trout

Oh, absolutely! I've seen it time and time again.

Wright

I've done so many different things in my life. I call it "genius."

Trout

Oh, I like that!

Wright

My wife calls it a character flaw. It's somewhere in the middle there. The real problem with it is, when someone asks, "What does David do?" for years she'd just say, "He's an entrepreneur." So one day, someone asked my now fourteen-year-old—when she was really little—that question and she said, "I think he's an entre-manure." So I think maybe she got closer to it.

Trout

She got closer to it. You know the hardest part about being an entrepreneur is it's so hard to explain who you are! People are so used to having people put in boxes, and there just ain't no box for us!

Wright

That's right!

Trout

It's a problem in some cases, because people really *need* to be able to settle in on something. You know, when I say to people, "Oh, I could be your photographer for that wedding." They look at me and I say, "Well, you know, I'm developing training and I'm photographing weddings." Huh? But

I ask, "Why not?" And then, "Oh yeah, you need a conference speaker? Well, sure, I'd love to. Happen to have a whole litany of topics I could speak on!"

Wright

What advice or recommendations would you have for leaders today and in the future?

Trout

First of all, you've got to accept it! If you *are* in a leadership role or if you see that people are coming to you *needing* a leader, accept it and realize that you have the ability to help people move forward. The difference between a leader and an average person is that an average person thinks in terms of making choices. It's like, "Oh, there's a choice here and there's a choice there..." Basically, they keep looking at all the choices. But leaders make decisions! Leaders help people see where they are moving. Groups and organizations *need* somebody to help them see that vision and to take that next step and to have the courage to do that. The other thing I tell people is, *study* leadership. Take your role seriously and learn how to do it better. Understand how to lead *well,* because there are models out there that can help us understand how to eliminate a lot of the consequences that poor leadership leads to.

Wright

Do you think that anyone can become a leader? And what's your definition of leadership success?

Trout

This is always one of those $64,000 questions. My opinion is that *most* people can rise to the occasion under a crisis, for a short term. For example, one day I was driving into town, and there was an accident at an intersection. Immediately, this biker dude jumped off his Harley and started directing traffic—really taking charge. He had long hair with a braid and a leather jacket and everything. I don't mean to say that he was in any way a bad person, but it is so interesting to see how people in crisis will jump forward and make something happen. But not very many people will get into it for the long haul and will attempt to really move a community or an organization forward and hang in there and see if they can do it over the duration. The long haul is much tougher, and I don't think anyone should assume that just anybody could do it.

It requires such a combination of talent and charisma and tenacity and persistence and confidence. Leaders have plenty of opportunity to get shaken. People come at you when you are the leader. It's not an easy role to play, and a lot of people prefer not to have to take on that kind of criticism or to be that vulnerable. So in the long run, if you're talking about leadership over the long haul, I don't think just anybody can do it. But people can learn to do it *better* if, once they're in that role, they decide to take responsibility for themselves.

Wright

So you are sitting as president of a national association committed to applied and therapeutic humor, you're completing a Ph.D., and you're holding down a corporate job.

Trout

Yes. So what's your point?

Wright

Do you ever have time to laugh right now?

Trout

Oh, I have to tell you, in spite of how crazy it sounds, I'm absolutely living a dream. I absolutely love my life right now. I'm getting to do things that I never ever dreamed I would get to do. I got my bachelor's degree when I was thirty-nine, and I didn't go back to school until I was thirty-five, because I really thought I wasn't bright enough to get a college degree to begin with. So to be getting a Ph.D. right now is just an unbelievable dream.

Working with a national organization and leading it through radical change is beyond my wildest dreams. And I have a great family. And you know, I *am* the president of a *therapeutic humor* organization, so I absolutely *have* to walk the talk. One of the things is that you have to model the way. I'm not laughing as much as I probably do when I don't have these kinds of responsibilities, but I can tell you that I am surrounded with great people who make sure that they lift *me* up. They send me things that are just hysterical to the situation. Yeah, I laugh. There's no doubt about it—I'm laughing. I'm just genuinely enjoying the journey.

Wright

What an interesting conversation! I really appreciate your talking to me today about such an important topic. I really learned, as a matter of fact, and I am going to check out your parenting book just to see if I've been doing it right for forty-one years.

Trout

I understand. I wrote *Light Dances* before my kids were all out of their teen years. And it is pretty poignant. You would enjoy it a lot. There are some pretty good pearls of wisdom in there.

Wright

I've had to learn three languages—the one that I communicated with *my* peers, the one that I communicated to the forty-one-year-old and the forty-year-old and now the language of my daughter. Of course, I don't say anything. I don't want her to think I'm stupid, you know.

Trout

Yes. I know, but you might as well. She's going to assume that for a few years here.

Wright

That's right. I really appreciate your being with us today. Today, we have been talking to Shirley Trout. She is a diverse professional communicator. She calls herself, "The Laughter-Learning Link," because she helps adults laugh while they are learning, and she helps children learn while they are laughing. What a great life job. Thank you so much, Shirley.

Trout

Thank *you*, David.

Shirley K. Trout
15500 Bluff Road
Waverly, NE 68462
Phone: 402.786.3100
Fax: 402.786.2131
Email: strout@teachablemoments.com
www.teachablemoments.com

Chapter 17

ELLEN SPENCER SUSMAN

After years as a television anchor-reporter, Ellen Spencer Susman now brings journalistic experience and perspective to you! Her innovative, monthly, live Internet conference, "Leaders Forum," provides leadership insight into corporate culture to clients as diverse as Land's End, Protective Life Insurance and The Veteran's Administration. An accomplished, solution-oriented speaker and moderator, Susman focuses on leadership, communication and women's issues.

David E. Wright (Wright)

Today, we're talking to Ellen Spencer Susman, the founder and moderator of Leader's Forum. She began her career in journalism as one of the original hosts of KYW-TV's evening *PM Magazine* in Philadelphia, Pennsylvania. After a successful career as a television news reporter and anchor, she created, produced and hosted a television show for The Aspen Institute in Aspen, Colorado, that focused on leadership issues with high-profile people in industry and government. That led to a series for Westcott Communications called *Experience Teaches*, which featured well-known business leaders such as Motorola's Bob Galvin and Warren Bennis in live, two-hour open-forum discussions with as many as 600 participants.

In 1997, Ellen created Leaders Forum as an executive education Internet program to provide insight into the world of leadership development for clients such as Land's End, the Veteran's Administration, Protective Life Insurance and others.

Ellen, welcome to *Taking Charge: Lessons in Leadership.*

Ellen Spencer Susman (Susman)

Thank you, David.

Wright

Could you share with me how you became interested in leadership?

Susman

I initially became interested in leadership because of the work I was do-ing at the Aspen Institute for Humanistic Studies in Aspen, Colorado. While interviewing some of the world's movers and shakers, I was also learning about the Institute's programs and discovered that the key phrase was val-ues-based leadership. The way they communicated this concept was through executive seminars, in which people reread the so-called great books and reflected on timeless ideas starting with Socrates and continuing through Martin Luther King, Jr. The ultimate goal for the participants was to integrate those combinations of beliefs and ideas into their own lives and promote dialogue. The notion of going to the past to better form the future fascinated me, along with the diverse and accomplished people.

Wright

Was values-based leadership the focus of Leader's Forum?

Susman

It was the focus of the Institute. When I was asked to create a long-distance executive education program for the Internet, I didn't even know if it could be done! The initial idea was to have business leaders share their ideas with upper-level managers so they could improve their capabilities. Another hook was that these were people that most upper-level managers would never usually have access to.

My take was that it was leadership from a leader's perspective with a journalistic slant.

Wright

Just to clarify for our readers, and for me, when you talk about values-based leadership, what is "values-based" being compared to? What other kind of leadership is there?

Susman

Good point! Well, the opposite of values is amorality. And since we're dealing with lessons in leadership, our concern is moral and ethical values. Those at the head of public, private or non-profit companies have an obligation to act in the best interests of their employees and shareholders. When you are at the top of the ladder, the people below model every action you take. So the accountability factor gets raised to a higher level the higher you go. As we've seen in the last few years, through Enron, Tyco, Global Crossing and others, when accountability fails, companies fail. That's leadership at its worst—what I call value-less leadership.

Wright

What lessons can be learned from Leader's Forum?

Susman

That's a hard one, since each one of our thirty-two guests had amazing take-away information. Leader's Forum has all of the interviews and slides that correspond to the talks in our archives at our Web site, www.leadersforum.com, so I urge people to visit and choose for themselves! After listening to various top executives and business authors speak out on topics ranging from changing corporate culture to communities of practice, the subject that comes up over and over again is the effort to manage change and what it takes to do that successfully. However, in terms of shaping today's leader, I would cite Steve Mercer, who is vice president of Learning and Leadership Development at Boeing. His task was to create the Boeing Leadership Center and an integral leadership development curriculum. Since it's Boeing, they have a fully integrated leadership flight simulator, in which people actually feel like they are running a business. Their executive program requires every one of their executives to attend a residential, twelve-day program. The philosophy is leaders teaching leaders and learning by doing. Mercer says the only failure at the leadership center is the failure to learn from your mistakes.

Steve Kerr, who is Chief Learning Officer at GE, says that good leaders are experts at breaking down communication barriers. Jim O'Toole, formerly of The Aspen Institute and now with Booz Allen Hamilton, says the most important thing he's learned while working with corporations is that although many companies have tremendous potential for improvement, in almost every case, the stumbling block is leadership. O'Toole says leaders have the vision, architecture and leadership needed to effectuate change. Still, it seems in some way that great leaders are born, not created.

Wright

Is executive education online a good learning tool?

Susman

I think it is an excellent tool, especially for companies in today's global workplace. It is time efficient and budget friendly. It allows many people to participate, is an easy way to share information in a concentrated setting and is controllable, because it is on company time.

Wright

Is it like a chat room?

Susman

That is a common misconception. It couldn't be further from a chat room. First of all, it is closed, except to participants. You have a call-in number through a phone router and a password to get into the site that is sent by our web master.

Wright

So you talk to a person, rather than being on a computer?

Susman

Yes. The computer is a tool for looking at the speaker's slides and visualizing the information that is being imparted. The dialogue is what is most valuable. In this situation, you can ask questions of an expert that are specific to your set of organizational problems. The end goal is to receive useful take-away information that can be applied to your work environment. I always felt that if everyone just got *one* thing they could use, the session was a success.

Wright

Real-time dialogue is the only way I've ever been able to learn much of anything.

Susman

A professor of classics once told me that your auditory senses shut down once you begin looking at things. When we put Leader's Forum together, we made a rule that guest speakers had to have their information to us ten days ahead of broadcast so attendees could download the information and absorb it. That way, the slides were secondary on session day and the participants had moved ahead into question mode about how this information affected them.

Wright

Do you think executive programs online will have a positive effect on future leaders?

Susman

I think it will be one of many tools that future leaders use to stay current and ahead of the curve. But don't discount the strength of people relating to and learning from people in person. If you need more executive education, this is a wonderful adjunct to the process. I think it's positive, because you get immediate feedback. But nothing is a substitute for hands-on learning.

Wright

Why are people so fascinated by leaders and leadership?

Susman

Leadership today is a hot topic! Figures indicate that there are approximately 1,700 books a year published under this heading. But I think people are fascinated for the wrong reasons. It appears that if you are a leader, you have money, power, fame and position. Our society craves that, and by the way, often confuses movie stars and athletes with leaders—which is wrong. They are personalities who are fame driven, not leadership driven. Real leaders come to the forefront when crises evolve, like Churchill or Gandhi or Mandela. Real leaders are out there getting everyone on the same page when the going gets really tough. One of the fascinations with leadership comes from the perception that they have something special, some quality that the rest of us don't have. They have the touch of immortality, and that is an awesome attribute.

Wright

What do great leaders do differently, and how do they take charge?

Susman

They communicate differently. Great leaders are able to cut to the chase, speak from the heart and the gut. They are able to focus on many issues and not get distracted from the key issue. They are able to coordinate various and diverse challenges. They just cope in a more finely tuned way. And finally, they have more energy. All of the people I've met who lead require less sleep than the rest of us. They have, as Professor Warren Bennis would say, competence, ambition and integrity. *Results-Based Leadership* by Ulrich, Smallwood and Zenger talks about competencies of characteristics of leadership. One of their key points is that admired leaders not only learn how to act but act in ways that ensure results. They claim that leadership attributes fall into three broad categories: who leaders are, what leaders know and what leaders do. I found that fascinating.

Wright

Have you ever seen a situation in business where the CEO was not the leader and someone else was?

Susman

Yes. But only in companies where the founder realized that his vision was sufficient but his organizational skills were not suitable to maintain the growth of the organization. In that situation, they remain the heart of the company culture until they step aside. At that point, the culture is morphing anyway since it's growing. A perfect example of this recently is Hewlett Packard, which had foundered since the deaths of the founders but was held together by memories. New leaders were at odds between the legacy and the immediate challenges of running a 21st century global company in a very competitive field.

Wright

In this era of CEO bashing, how do you suggest we separate the wheat from the chaff when it comes to leaders?

Susman

There is a very good book called *Good to Great* by Jim Collins, which correlates economic performance and CEO attributes. He says that CEOs who build great teams and put company achievement above personal fame are more likely to produce great results that are sustained over the long haul. That rings very true, because the influence from the stock market on valuation and economic forecasts has put CEOs in a difficult position. There is such a push for immediate results, and everything happens at such speed that there is little chance to reflect and make hard decisions slowly. Any well-grounded business person will tell you that the process of growing a company is slow, and it can easily take years for a management team to develop sound strategies, let alone implement them. So Collins is right: Good CEOs build teams, build loyalty, communicate their ideas and then see good bottom-line performance. So again, it's that combination of ambition, competence and integrity that separates poor, good and great leaders.

Wright

Can you tell me the difference, as you perceive it, between a leader and a great manager?

Susman

Of course, it is my perception, but the main difference between great managers and leaders all comes down to communication. Professor John Adair of Sandhurst Military School in England looks at leadership as a three-ringed, interlocking circle of task, individual and team. First, he says, know your task. Second, deal with the individual and give him or her attention. Third, deal with the team. And this almost perfectly defines the difference. Good managers understand task and team but are weak on the individual. Leaders understand task, team *and* individual. So communication is the key.

Wright

What do you see as the biggest challenges facing leaders in the 21st century?

Susman

We have multiple challenges ahead in this new century! One of the biggest is intolerance—the threat of different religions, fanatics, people who are uncomfortable with the role of women and blacks in society. One challenge was brought to my attention at a Yale University School of Management panel discussion about 21st century leaders. One of the participants, Indra Nooyi, had just been named as CEO of PepsiCo. As the parent of a young son, she disclosed that when she made the decision to take the job, her husband agreed that he would be the primary caregiver to the child. Balancing work and life is one of the biggest obstacles facing leaders today—not only balancing your own work and family life providing that for your employees. It is essential to success, however you measure it, to have your work life complement your home life. It is changing. Many companies provide child care, more are trying flextime with employees, and many are job sharing. That's a big help. As society continues to change and there are more career couples, all of these issues will find their level.

Wright

Do you think it will be better for our culture?

Susman

I hope so. I think it is terrible that women are so often forced to choose between their career and their children. I think in the best of all worlds and situations, organizations would realize that it is a waste of time and training to lose talent over a biological fact. The best course for our culture would be to reward people for balancing their families and jobs—not force them to choose one or the other!

Wright

The only problem with changing culture is that people want to go back to "the good ole days," which will never happen, because the world keeps changing. I guess it's better to adapt and find methods to accommodate our cultural changes, like the woman at PepsiCo.

Susman

Well, we also have to say that the "good ole days" are here and now. We live in a vibrant and exciting time that is in constant flux. We all have the ability to make the best of ourselves. Actually, I wouldn't want to be anywhere else.

Wright

Spoken like a happy person on her job, which is surprising when you read statistics like eighty-seven percent of people in America go to work somewhere they don't want to be. You're not one of those people.

Susman

I'm not. I love my life, and I think you can work to change what you're unhappy with. Take a course, read a book, follow your dream. The people who are happy in life aren't afraid to shake it up and try new things.

Take Peter Drucker. He continues, in his nineties, to write about business. The great leadership expert, Warren Bennis, who has spent his whole life studying this subject, doesn't stick with the opinions he came up with in the '60s! Great leaders learn from others!

Wright

I guess evolving is the key.

Susman

That's lessons in leadership. We can learn from everyone around us and remember that good leaders communicate!

Wright

What an interesting conversation. I appreciate the time you've spent with me. I've learned a lot, and I'm certain our readers have as well.

Susman

I hope so. I enjoyed talking with you.

Wright

We've been talking with Ellen Spencer Susman. She is the moderator of Leader's Forum, an Internet conference, and, as we've learned, knows a lot about leadership. Thank you so much, Ellen, for being with us.

Susman

Thank you so much, David.

Ellen Spencer Susman
2121 Kirby Drive
Houston, TX 77019
Phone: 713.522.7745
Mobile: 713.501.8884
Fax: 713.522.5157
Email: esusman@earthlink.net
www.leadersforum.com
www.superwomancentral.com